Me & Patsy Kickin' Up Dust

Also by Loretta Lynn

Honky Tonk Girl: My Life in Lyrics

You're Cooking It Country: My Favorite Recipes and Memories

Still Woman Enough: A Memoir

Loretta Lynn: Coal Miner's Daughter

Me & Patsy Kickin' Up Dust

My Friendship with Patsy Cline

Loretta Lynn

with Patsy Lynn Russell

Foreword by Dolly Parton

GRAND CENTRAL PUBLISHING

New York Boston

Cover design by Phil Pascuzzo
Cover photos: (Lynn) Michael Ochs Archives / Handout; (Patsy) Patsy Cline Enterprises, LLC

Grand Central Publishing
Hachette Book Group
1290 Avenue of the Americas, New York, NY 10104
grandcentralpublishing.com
twitter.com/grandcentralpub

First edition: April 2020

Grand Central Publishing is a division of Hachette Book Group, Inc. The Grand Central Publishing name and logo is a trademark of Hachette Book Group, Inc.

Book designed by Marie Mundaca

Library of Congress Control Number: 2019954480

ISBNs: 978-1-5387-0166-9 (hardcover), 978-1-5387-5214-2 (large print), 978-1-5387-0167-6 (ebook)

Printed in the United States of America

LSC-H

10 9 8 7 6 5 4 3 2 1

I would like to dedicate this book to Charlie and Patsy's children, Julie and Randy. You were Daddy and Mommy's whole heart.

And to my children, who are mine: Betty, Jack, Ernest, Cissie, Peggy, and Patsy.

I also dedicate this book to all the women out there who haven't yet found their special friendship. Keep looking—it's out there.

For those of you who have, love your friend the best you can. Don't waste a second.

To my daughter, Patsy. There is no one I would rather have wrote the story of me and Patsy with. Now, go tell it. I love you.

Contents

Foreword

Friendship is important, but a friendship between two women is always great. I'm so happy that Loretta and Patsy had that. I have had a best friend, Judy Ogle, for sixty-plus years, and there's nothing like someone knowing exactly who you are, who you were, who you want to be. It's nice to be able to be as open and honest with someone else as you are with yourself. I think friendship is a wonderful thing, and it's beautiful that women can have and share that kind of relationship. There's nobody like my best friend Judy, and I'm sure that's how Patsy and Loretta felt.

There is not a person in the music industry who does not feel like Patsy Cline and Loretta Lynn blazed a trail for the rest of us to follow. With their distinct voices, memorable lyrics, and emotional stories, they set the tone for what all musicians aspire to—to this day. *Nobody* else sounds like Loretta, and *nobody* else sounds like Patsy.

The first time I heard Patsy Cline's voice, it really caught my ear. She is a true stylist, and I just thought it was so very different and so unusual. I have always loved her sound. I'm a great admirer of people who have developed their own style. My favorite song of Patsy's was "Walkin' After Midnight." It was haunting and special and painted a picture that I will never forget. I know the fans loved the song "Crazy," which I did as well, but we all have our favorites. Just like "Coat of Many Colors" is my favorite song that I've written, "Coal Miner's Daughter" is my favorite song of Loretta's. Everybody loves a story song, and I think Loretta is a true storyteller.

I got to know Loretta because we were both girl singers, so to speak, on two of the biggest-ever syndicated country music shows: *The Wilburn Brothers Show* and *The Porter Wagoner Show*. Sometimes I feel like we eclipsed our male counterparts, which caused friction. We drew our own fans, and I think we both kind of knew that. I think we could both smile with each other and say, "Hey, girl, we're doin' all right, ain't we?!" Even though Porter Wagoner and the Wilburn Brothers had been good enough to give us a break and a chance, and we both appreciated and respected that, we were very proud of ourselves and of each other for being able to withstand all that we did and to just stand up there with the best of them.

I think it's wonderful that women are doing great in country music. There were a few of us back then, and there's many more of us now. I'm hoping that country music will always open its doors, arms, hearts, and minds to all the young and upcoming women. Any woman with talent who has the desire and the ability to do it should be given the chance and the opportunity.

Women are trying to stick tighter together more than ever, especially with this new wave of female singers that is coming along now. I think it's flattering that they refer to me, Loretta, and Patsy as their inspiration. The fact that they're sticking together as women and trying to gain strength in numbers is always helpful. I'm all for the girls. I'm there for you.

—Dolly Parton

Me & Patsy Kickin' Up Dust

Writing My Feelings

Hello, everybody. I'm Loretta Lynn.

Most people know me as a country music singer. I've been singing for as long as I can remember. Seems to me I could sing before I could talk. I have a lot of fans and I love every single one. But the truth is I'd rather be writing than singing for a crowd. Writing songs is part of who I am, down deep. It comes natural as havin' a baby, which I can tell you ain't easy. I've had six! Putting words to feelings is a lot like that—it's hard but worth every minute of pain. I started when I was a young woman, singing for my babies, and I ain't done yet.

I've wrote a lot of songs—over 150, but people don't think of me right off when it comes to books. Maybe it's 'cause I'm not what you'd call educated. But this ain't my first book. That was *Coal Miner's Daughter*. I was barely forty-three when I wrote that with a fella named George Vecsey—half the age I am now. Seems funny to think I had a life story to tell yet, but that book became a *New York Times* best seller. Then, after my husband died, I had some things

I wanted to set straight, so I wrote *Still Woman Enough*, and that book was a *New York Times* best seller, too.

So why write another book at my age? I'm glad to tell you. See, once upon a time I met this woman, a few months older than me, by the name of Patsy Cline. Likely as anything you know her music, and if you don't, well, you should. Patsy was a popular country music singer. When I first came to Nashville, just a bashful young mother and hoping to make my way in the country music business, she reached out to me. She took me under her wing and became one of my greatest friends in this whole world. She died when we were both still so young. We were here way before Nashville was the destination it is nowadays, with hundreds of thousands of fans coming to see country music artists perform. It was just a little town, really. Me and Patsy bonded close as sisters. As time has gone on, I haven't stopped loving Patsy or thinking about her and talking to her, even. Not for one single day. She changed my life forever.

Patsy Cline taught me a bunch that I'll want to share. Things like how to dress for the stage, how to stand up for myself, how to fight for what's right, and even how to spice up my love life. (I've been holding back telling that story for a long time. Just wait'll you hear it!)

But most of all, Patsy was my confidante and friend. We cooked together, chased after our kids together, helped each other around the house, and talked about our husbands like girlfriends do. I want folks to know how good Patsy was—and not just good at making music, though she was amazing at that for sure. Her voice still sounds like an angel's to me.

Patsy was the real deal. People throw around the word *authentic* a lot. But ask anyone who knew her and they'll tell you Patsy Cline was the most real person you could ever meet. With her, it was always what you see is what you get. That's one reason we got along so good. When people are fake, I just can't stand it! Patsy didn't pretend about nothing. She was as real as it gets. So I'm gonna share stories about our time together. Along the way, maybe I'll encourage people to listen to her music. Patsy had the richest, most emotional voice you ever heard. There are lots of her songs worth listening to.

People ask me for advice about how to make it in the music business. Here's what Patsy taught me: Nobody can tell you who you are. Ain't nobody can be you but you. Work hard and stay true to yourself. That's it, pure and simple. It's hard as hell to make it in this business. You gotta work your ass off, and hard work is rare these days. Just 'cause you've got a nice voice or good looks, that don't mean you're gonna get a hit and be rich and famous. I'm sorry. That ain't happening. Success don't happen overnight. Scratch that. There have been a few one-hit wonders.

The truth is, if you have a girlfriend on your side, somebody who knows the real you and believes in you, no matter what, it can make all the difference in the world. It did for me. Patsy was that friend. We understood each other and we had each other's backs. When you have a friend like that, it changes you. It gives you strength and gives you faith in yourself. That kind of friendship means more than anything. If you don't have one, I hope you'll open your heart to find one. Everybody deserves their own Patsy Cline.

Some people say that Patsy and I changed country music for the good of all women who come after us. I am not bragging on myself, but it makes me deeply proud to hear that. How did we change country music? I guess because we were the first to kick down the golden country music doors. Patsy shut up all those folks who said women can't sell tickets or records. She was the first female country singer to cross over to the pop and adult contemporary charts. She introduced millions of folks to country music and got people who loved her songs to listen to other country artists. She was also one of the first women to headline and sell out her own concerts. And she was the first female to headline in Vegas.

These changes in the early 1960s were major victories for us girls! Back then, Patsy didn't even realize the path she was clearing for all of us to follow. But if it wasn't for the strides Patsy Cline made for us, then I don't know if I would have been able to accomplish all my own firsts, like how I was the first female to ever win the CMA Entertainer of the Year Award and then the first to do it again at the ACM Awards three years later. Those two awards mean so much to me, because they helped every girl singer who came after to stop thinking it couldn't happen for them. Because, friends, if I, Loretta Lynn from Butcher

Holler, Kentucky—the one they called a hillbilly and made so much fun of, a working wife and mother of six kids—could bring home the highest honor that could be given in country music, well, then maybe they had some hope themselves.

As I have said many, many times: To make it you have to be first, great, or different. Between the two of us, I believe Patsy and I had all three covered, and she brought out the best in me and I like to think I helped bring out the best in her, too. Now, did we change country music? Well, you better believe we did!

I named my daughter after Patsy. That's how much she meant to me. When I had my twins the year after Patsy died, I named them Peggy and Patsy. If only Patsy had been there for that. She'd have liked it. I traveled so much that I didn't get to spend much time with the twins when they were growing up, but these days me and my daughter Patsy are real close. She's heard all my stories about Patsy Cline. How could I even say the name Patsy without thinking of her? After a while, my Patsy said, "Mommy, we got to get some of these stories down." I knew she was right.

So that's why you hold this here book in your hands. Putting it together has been bittersweet. It's hurt some, and I've cried more than a few times—kinda like when I write a good song. It's been real good for my soul. I hope you enjoy it as much as I've loved putting it together for you.

—Loretta Lynn, Nashville, 2019

Sitting Up with the Dead

I walked into Patsy Cline's house on Nella Drive like I always did, without knocking.

My husband, Doo, carried in the food we'd brought and laid it out in the kitchen. Already there was enough to feed an army: fried chicken, baked ham, deviled eggs, biscuits, pies, cakes. And, of course, drinks: Cokes and beer and liquor. You'd have thought it was another one of her and Charlie's famous parties.

Things looked the same, but there was something off in that house. I told myself it was because Patsy wasn't there to greet me like usual, hollerin', "It's about time you got here, Little Gal!" But there was something else: There wasn't no music playin'. When Patsy had folks over, there'd always be a radio on, a record spinning, or tapes on the reel-to-reel. Patsy listened to all kinds of music. She'd opened my eyes to blues and R&B and swing. I remember she played me Etta James singing "At Last." I was amazed. I loved it!

Now it was too quiet. People was talking, but they was

hushed. Patsy liked to talk loud, and whenever she was holdin' court, the room would be filled with laughter, too. That day the sounds were all wrong in there, seemed like.

I started helping right away, carving up a ham, trying to be useful. Guests were arriving already—the house would be packed before long. But my brain was foggy, and I was in shock. All I could think was, *This can't be right. Patsy's too young to die.* Hell, we were both just thirty, born a few months apart, her in Virginia and me in the hills of Kentucky. There was so much living left to do for both of us. Julie and Randy, her two little kids, needed raising. And Patsy's dreams had just started to come true! She was winning all kinds of awards, and folks from all over were hearing her music on the radio, getting to know how special Patsy Cline was. How could she be gone from this world?

When there wasn't no more food left to prepare, I went on into the living room, where her gold casket was on display in front of the big picture window. The drapes were closed. It was chilly for March. *Maybe poor Charlie forgot to turn on the heat*, I thought. He had a lot going on. I stood by the casket, wishing I could see Patsy one more time, but the lid was closed. The plane crash had been too awful to leave it open. Charlie'd put Patsy's best publicity picture on top. She smiled in that picture like she didn't have a care in the world.

This wasn't nothing like the sittin'-up ceremonies we had in the hills. Back home, when somebody died the body'd be laid out, not boxed up. We used to sit up with a body for days, singing and crying. How else could you get used to the idea of a soul going to heaven? Hilda, Patsy's momma, planned to have the funeral back in Virginia and bury her there. That would have ticked Patsy off. She used to say, "The next time I set foot in Winchester, everybody in town'll know Patsy Cline has been there!" Well, at least that'd be true now.

I sat down on the pretty white sofa Patsy'd had made special. In my mind, I couldn't stop fussing over her. Had they done her makeup good? Patsy hated when her scars showed. They better have had the sense to put her in a good dress. Patsy wore the prettiest clothes, real sophisticated. She'd grown out of the cowgirl look she wore all those years ago when she was just getting started. She gave away a bunch of those costumes and ordered fancy dresses and long gowns special. Nobody could call Patsy Cline a "hillbilly" anymore. She was too elegant. She didn't care what folks expected of her. To hell with what anybody else thinks, she said. She wanted to feel good.

Most everybody else was in the kitchen, drinking and eating. I was sad and mad at the same time that nobody but me was sitting with Patsy in that living room that she'd fixed up so nice and pretty. So I decided to stay with her a bit, just me and her, like we'd done so many times before. I thought, *What am I gonna do now? I don't have nobody to take care of me or fight for me anymore.*

Right then I felt a cold chill—goose bumps running up my arms. I shivered and said out loud, "Dadgum, it's cold in here!" Like I said, there wasn't nobody to hear me so I don't know why I said it out loud. But then I heard Patsy's voice, like she was right next to me. She said, "Well, turn on the damn heat!" I swear I heard her plain as day. So I got up and did just that.

Funny thing was, I was glad. Patsy was still tellin' me what to do. Since the day we met, she'd been saying I could do something to change things, encouraging me to stand up for myself and for my music. Whatever it was, she always told me the God's honest truth and she always had my back. She'd said I could do it and she was right. Patsy hadn't left me. I would keep hearing her voice, in the days and the weeks after her death. Even now, years later, I still hear her. She came into my life and changed everything. And I know I meant a lot to her, too. She'll always be a part of me. That's what real friendships do. We made each other better.

That Girl's Gonna Be Somebody

The first time I ever laid eyes on Patsy Cline, it was 1957. I was in the front room at the little farmhouse where me and my husband, Oliver "Mooney" Lynn, lived in Custer, Washington. I'd been working all day at Bob and Clyde Green's dairy farm. I cleaned, washed, ironed, and cooked for the thirty-six ranch hands that worked there. My husband worked there, too. He'd milk the cows in the mornings, work in the fields all day, then milk again in the evening. I always called him Doo—short for Doolittle—but he was a hard worker. We both were—always have been. That's why the Greens let us live in a little house out there on their farm. I was maybe twenty-four at the time and already had four kids. I guess Ernie would have been about three, Cissie was five, Jack was maybe eight, and Betty Sue was nine.

Me and Doo didn't have much, but we'd scraped together some money and got us a black-and-white television set from Sears and Roebuck. That was a big deal. We put a payment down, then paid something every month—took about forever to finally own that thing. It was a black-and-white television set with two big wire antennas on the top. You'd wiggle those around just right until you got a signal comin' in good. This was way before cable or even color televisions. We had about two stations that'd come in good enough to watch. We'd just turn that thing on and watch whatever we could get. We thought we were ridin' high.

You might laugh—even to me it sounds a little funny now, with people watching shows on their phones on airplanes or standing in line waiting for their coffees at the Starbucks. Back then television was something new, something different. People'd come from miles to watch a TV. Wasn't no shame in it. We were all poor. We sat on the floor watching. No carpet or nothing. We just barely had a wood floor. Listen, we were poor people.

That night the Arthur Godfrey show came on—*Arthur Godfrey's Talent Scouts*, it was called. That's the first time I ever seen Patsy. When she come on, boy, it caught my eye. I couldn't take my eyes off her. She sung like she was singing just for one person watchin'. She sang "Walkin' After Midnight." Her voice was so powerful. So rich and pretty with a real lonesome sound. I didn't know their names yet, but there was Grady Martin and Hank "Sugarfoot" Garland on guitar and Owen Bradley on piano next to her, just a-smilin'. She wasn't nothing like any of the other girl singers I'd ever heard. Her singing like to break my heart. I thought, *That girl's gonna be somebody.*

I had a real good feelin' about Patsy Cline. I felt real proud of her somehow, like we were connected, even though we'd never met. See, not long before I saw Patsy sing on Arthur Godfrey's show, I'd started singing myself.

We'd been married about ten years when Doo figured out I could sing. He'd heard me singing for the kids and said I sounded pretty good. In 1957, he surprised me with a seventeen-dollar Harmony guitar that I taught myself to play. Wasn't much else to do besides cook and clean and chase after the kids. Besides, making music was something I'd always done. I wasn't too good at chores and, with eight kids, Mommy'd made sure we all pulled our own weight. So I'd make myself useful rockin' and singin' to the young 'uns. I remember one night rocking my baby brother on the porch, just a singin'. Daddy hollered, "Pipe down, Loretta! Everybody on the mountain can hear you!" I hollered back, "Don't matter. They're all our cousins!"

Wasn't nothing special about me being able to sing. My whole family did. Mommy had a beautiful voice—much prettier'n mine. When I was little I'd sneak out of my bed to hear my parents sing and play the banjo. Daddy could play anything. Mommy could, too. Mommy taught me songs like "The Great Titanic." Most of our songs told a story. That's how folks shared the news, with songs. We didn't have newspapers or televisions. And we sang hymns. Our family went to church when we could. We sang "How Great Thou Art" and "Where No One Stands Alone." I was a tenderhearted child, and I liked songs that made me cry. I still get choked up at "The Old Rugged Cross."

When I started learning to play that guitar, I got a copy of *Country Song Roundup* to learn the words to all the country hits on the radio. I looked at the songs in there and thought, *Anybody can do this*. I wrote my own songs to play. I wrote about things that happened, things that I felt—about raisin' babies, about love and family, and about my feelings. I wrote about marriage and betrayal and hurt. Being able to write about things I felt deep inside was good. And when Doo heard the songs I wrote, he said they were good. Doo hadn't ever encouraged me like that. I liked it.

Doo worked pretty regular, but we were barely living on what he made. Somehow he decided my singin' was our ticket. He started acting like maybe I was worth more than just a woman he lived with, having his babies and cookin' his supper. I won't lie. I liked it when he saw me that way. It made me think maybe there was more to me, too. After that, me and Doo were a team. No matter what, me and Doo were gonna make something out of ourselves, for our family. He'd say, "There's a bar down the road and you're going to learn a song and talk to the man and make him let you get up there and sing." And I'd do it, or we'd do it together.

Doo believed in me and he pushed me. He'd say, "I think you're that good." And I'd listen, because I trusted him. Most of the time he was right, and you don't disrespect that kind of dedication.

Without Doo, I'd never have even thought to get paid for singing. Where I grew up, folks made their money workin' in the mines. Or they ran moonshine, maybe. Making music was just something to pass the time and please yourself. Besides, like I told Doo, I just wanted to sing for my kids. I didn't need nobody else to hear. But Doo said, "Trust me." He'd been around the world. He knew better than me. Besides, I didn't go to bars to hear live music. But Doo? He'd been to his fair share of honky-tonks. More than his fair share, really.

At first I didn't want to do it. But when Doo got an idea in his head, he was bullheaded. I begged and cried and tried to get out of performing in front of people, but he wouldn't let me. He forced me to go onstage and sing. It was a struggle. I did it 'cause he made me. At first playing for a crowd made me want to turn and run, but Doo wouldn't let me. So I kept at it. And after a while I got to where I loved performing. And when folks liked the songs I'd wrote, it made it even better. It sparked something in me. Something good.

Doo wasn't a bit bashful about promotin' me. He'd walk right in and say, "You ever heard of Kitty Wells?" 'Course they'd say yes, 'cause Kitty was the first female country music star. She had the first number one hit by a woman, in 1952. Doo would say, "Well, I got the best girl singer you ever heard next to Kitty Wells." That'd get their attention. But they'd usually say, "Bring her over and we'll let her audition." Doo wouldn't let up. He'd say, "Naw, Loretta's the best. You're gonna want her onstage tonight!" Doo pushed me. I'd have never made it if he hadn't. I was too bashful. That might be hard to believe, but it's true.

So that's what was going on in the back of my mind when I saw Patsy sing on TV. She was as good as Hank

Williams, maybe better—and she was a woman! That was a new thing, newer than television, maybe even. The audience loved her. On Arthur Godfrey's show it was the applause that told who won the contest. A little meter showed whether folks were clapping hard or not. When Patsy sang, that arrow went right to the top of the dial! I'd of voted for her, too, if I wasn't three thousand miles away. When she won, I remember Mr. Godfrey asked if she was happy. Patsy said, "Happy as if I had good sense." I remember chuckling at that. She was funny, and that made me like her even more.

I learned "Walkin' After Midnight" right away after that. I got the single when it come out. It wasn't just me that loved it. That song went to number two on the country charts. Patsy wasn't real country like I was used to. She was from the South, but she didn't talk like it. She loved country western music, though. She coulda sung whatever she wanted to. She coulda sung opera or jazz or anything. I guess country music DJs didn't care one way or the other because "Walkin' After Midnight" hit the country music charts and crossed over to the pop charts. It got to number twelve on the pop chart. It was real unusual for country songs to do that in those days. Just goes to show what a hit it was.

I didn't know any of that at the time. I just knew a good song when I heard one.

I didn't have a band then. Doo got me to sing with a local band called the Westerners at first. Then they got tired of paying me five dollars a show. My brother Jay Lee came from Kentucky to live with us in Washington state. So we got him and the steel guitar player named Roland Smiley from the Westerners to be my band. We called ourselves "Loretta and the Trail Blazers." Jay Lee'd joked they were really Loretta Lynn's Tail Riders, 'cause he said I rode 'em all the time. He was teasin', though. I didn't ride 'em. They knew how to play. Jay played the fiddle and the electric guitar. He'd lay one down and pick the other one up. I called Roland "Smiley Old Steel" 'cause he smiled all the time. Tickled him to death—he loved it.

After I worked up "Walkin' After Midnight" pretty good on my guitar, me and the boys played it around town. We worked up a lot of Patsy's songs. We played 'em at Bill's Tavern in Blaine, Washington, where Doo got me in to do the show every Saturday night.

Soon Doo had me performing everywhere—taverns, dance halls, and local radio shows. Patsy's singing inspired me. I started thinkin' maybe Doo was right. Maybe I could be a professional singer. I saved up some money from my Saturday night shows and bought me a pair of white Acme boots, a Western shirt, a skirt with a fringe on it, and a white cowgirl hat. I'd wear that anytime I'd sing for shows. Hell, I looked like a real cowgirl. Annie Oakley couldn't hold a candle to me.

In some of the old pictures of Patsy, you can see her wearing that same Western look with the fringes and the white hat. Maybe we were more alike than I knew. But I never dreamed I'd ever meet Patsy in person. She was famous, successful, and far, far away on the other side of the country in Nashville, Tennessee.

A Couple of Good Breaks out West

It's no secret that me and Doo had a rocky relationship from the start. I wasn't but a girl when we got married, then we moved across the country to Washington state with me seven months pregnant. Shoot, I never even been kissed before Doo. I took to mothering quicker than I took to being a wife. And Doo ran around on me from the start, drinking and carrying on with other women. He denied it to the end, but I know better. He did. Plenty of times.

After I got to singing pretty regular, Doo decided to get me on Buck Owens's television show. Buck was a country music singer just gettin' started. He had a show out of Tacoma. Doo went right to him and told him I should be on his show. So Buck let me sing onstage out at the Pantania Club. It wasn't a very nice place—I remember that. He let me sing one song. And then another. After that, he told Doo we should stay over for his show that Saturday night and he'd let me be on his radio show for the amateur competition night. Well, there were thirty other singers, but guess who won. Me! So I started to think, *Well, I must have a little something since I won that*. Doo thought I could make it as a singer, too, so I wasn't gonna argue.

Besides, I'd started making a little money for once. For the thirteen years I'd been living in Washington I never had two nickels to rub together. So many times I'd thought about leaving Doo, packing up the kids and heading back East. We had a lot of problems and let me tell you, too much money weren't one of 'em! But how could I leave? I didn't have any money. Every bit of work I did on the Greens' farm was so we didn't have to pay rent. Doo got paid cash and he considered that money his. He did whatever he wanted and dared me to say anything about it.

So the only time I ever had cash of my own was during strawberry-picking season, just a few weeks a year. Strawberry pickers got paid by the carrier. When you had eight quarts of berries, you'd take your ticket to Mr. Ernest Crandall for cash payment. I remember this one time me and Doo was having troubles again. When I went to cash in my ticket Mr. Ernest wouldn't give me the money! He knew me and Doo were in a big fight and he figured I'd take the money and leave Doo. I probably would've. I cooled off after a few days, so Mr. Crandall paid me.

After I started earning five dollars a Saturday night over at Bill's Tavern just for singing, I got to feelin' pretty good. It was my first real taste of freedom. And it came from me singing my songs. I liked that.

Another good thing about me going on Buck Owens's show was that I met Norm Burley. Mr. Burley was a successful businessman from Vancouver, Canada. He heard me sing a song I'd wrote called "Whispering Sea," and he told me it really got to him. He'd lost his wife and just wanted to listen to that song over and over. He said he wanted to invest in me and make a record of "Whispering Sea." I was so excited! I went home and wrote a bunch more songs right away.

Mr. Burley signed me as his first artist on the Zero Records label—a company he formed just to record me. He gave me and Doo the money to record a single.

Doo and me left the kids with my brother and his wife and drove on down to Los Angeles. We didn't know a thing about how to get a record made. Doo just knocked on doors 'til he found the studio where Speedy West worked. Speedy was well known in country music. He produced my first record. He got some real good musicians to play on it, too. We recorded "Whispering Sea" and "I'm a Honky Tonk Girl," a song I wrote about a girl I'd seen in Bill's Tavern. I'd seen this girl in there cryin' and drinkin' beer a bunch of times. I got to wonderin' about her story and I wrote that song.

Speedy did a good job producing them songs. He's the one put the drums in there. I didn't know it then, but Nashville country music producers wasn't using drums much. That gave my record a swinging little sound, I think.

A few weeks later, they shipped us those records. It was February 1960. I couldn't believe my songs were on an LP album! Me and Doo got right to work. We mailed out 3,500 copies with my picture to every country music radio station we could find. We called up disc jockeys and asked them to play "I'm a Honky Tonk Girl." Then Mr. Burley paid for us to go on a promotional trip. He was real good to us. We left the kids with my brother and his wife, and Doo drove our old Mercury down the West Coast and all over. It was the disc jockeys who decided what to play, so we got a list of those country DJs and hit every station on that list. Plus I'd perform anywhere they'd have me sing. Doo wasn't bashful to ask!

I just had one good dress, so I'd put it on in the car before I had to be somewhere to talk or sing. Then I'd change back into jeans when I got back in the car. To save money we slept in the car at night. You could do that in those days. We drove for weeks, sleeping in the car, eating so many baloney sandwiches I thought I'd die. But Doo said that's what we had to do to get people to buy my record. And he was right. By the summer of 1960, "I'm a Honky Tonk Girl" was number fourteen on the country charts!

Nashville Boys

While we were promoting that little record, me and Doo went to a radio convention out West. That's where I met Doyle and Teddy Wilburn, the duo called the Wilburn Brothers. They had a record deal with Decca Records, plus they had their own talent agency, the Wil-Helm Talent Agency. We hit it off right away. Them boys gave me their address and said if I ever came to Nashville I ought to look them up. Well, as soon as I got back to Custer, I wrote them a letter telling them how great it was to meet them. I also asked questions about Nashville—how to get my record sold, how to write the best songs—you name it, I asked. Doo had me include a copy of my record and my press photo, too.

I told the Wilburns that I hoped maybe someday I'd be on the Grand Ole Opry. For those of you ain't heard of it, it's a country music stage concert—the longest-running radio show in American history. It's been on broadcast every Saturday night since 1927. I've been listening to the Opry since I was eleven years old. That's when Daddy bought a transistor radio. It was during the war and batteries were hard to come by, so Daddy kept it off most of the time. But come Saturday night at eight, he'd tune in to WSM radio to the Grand Ole Opry. We'd all gather 'round to hear what they used to call "hillbilly music." There'd be something like ten different performers, with old favorites mixed in with the new. They played ballads, honky-tonk tunes, Gospel tunes, bluegrass, you name it. Sometimes Mommy would get moved by the music, then she'd pop up and dance. We kids loved that. Daddy'd put his head down, but I could see him grinning. I'd lay there with my head right up next to the speaker, listening to the Opry until I fell asleep.

Now I was dreaming about maybe singing on the Grand Ole Opry myself. I hadn't dreamed much for myself before. This was new. And I liked it.

The Wilburns wrote me right back. They said I had a lot of promise as a recording artist and they loved that I wrote my own songs. Back then songwriting was still a man's world. Girl singers didn't write their own songs. They said to keep writing! As for how I could get on the Opry show, they said since I already had a hit record on the country charts, I had a good chance. When I read that, I started yelling so loud! I scared Doo and the kids half to death. The Wilburns also said they'd send me some of the publishing company's songs and if I liked them, I could learn them. Then if Doo and I came to Nashville, well, Teddy'd cut a demo of me singing. I wrote back right away. I was so excited! My handwriting was a mess. It never was any good so I don't know how they even read the darn thing. Somehow they did and they wrote back right away with a tape of six songs and the lyrics. Their letter said, "Keep in touch. Hope you like the songs." Like 'em? Heck, I'd have learned to sing 'em in Chinese if I had to!

Doolittle thought I was too excited. He said, "Heck, Loretta. You don't know if these folks are just being nice to us or what!" But I did know, deep in me. This was the break we needed to get into the music business in Nashville. I didn't have a chance of making it out in Washington state. Nashville was where we needed to be.

So I worked on those six songs, day and night. I could sing 'em backwards and forwards. I dreamed about those songs. I'll never forget that one of 'em was written by a young man named Bobby Bare. He went on to be a big country music performer himself as well as a great songwriter.

Finally Doo decided it was time to make the move to Nashville. He said we needed to strike while the iron was hot. But first we had to talk with our Zero Records head, Mr. Burley. Listen, back then I was as green as you can be. I didn't know that most businessmen are all about how much money they can make off of you. Mr. Burley, though, he really loved me and Doo. He said the best way for me to make it as an artist was to let me go—and not just to Nashville. He told Doo, "If Loretta can get one of those big record companies to sign her on their label, I won't hold her back. She is free and clear to do so." Can you believe that? It was one of the kindest acts of love anyone had ever shown us.

So we contacted Doo's mommy and daddy, who were still in Kentucky, and my mommy, who was living in Wabash, Indiana. We told them all about our plans to move to Nashville. They agreed to watch the kids while Doo and I got settled there. Just as soon as Doo got a job and we found a place to live, we'd send for 'em. So it was almost all settled.

Clyde and Bob Green had taken Doo and me in and loved us like their own. They were the last people we had left to tell. It was so sad to even think of leaving the Greens' farm. It had been our home for so many years. Even though I was born in Kentucky, I've never loved anyplace the way I loved living in Washington state. Washington was home. I tell people that all the time. My first four kids say this, too. They loved being raised there. My son Ernest Ray and I talk all the time about going back. Maybe we will someday. Clyde and Bob were upset about losing us. Heck, they wanted me to leave young Jack Benny. He wasn't but eleven then, but they said they wanted to leave him the whole farm one day. Jack Benny loved it there and they didn't have a son, but I told them, "I can't leave my son. I just cain't." As much as it hurt us all, Clyde and Bob knew going to Nashville was the best thing we could do if I wanted to be a singer.

We packed up our old car and, after a river of tears, we set off east. I think back now and wonder how all six of us fit into that car. Lord, we must have been a sight. We only had enough money to get us to my mommy's in Wabash, Indiana. We stayed there just long enough for Doo to work some and earn some money. Cissie and Ernest stayed back with my mommy and we went on to Kentucky. After a night or two at Doo's mommy's, we left Jack and Betty behind and set off to Nashville. We were so excited, never even thinking of not making it. We didn't have no backup plan and not much money, so we had to make something happen. We never even thought of going back. Not ever.

So that's how, in 1959, we rolled into Nashville in Doo's old Mercury. Nashville was more a town than a city—not near as big as it is now—but it sure seemed big to me. Already it was the biggest recording center outside New York and Los Angeles. I was wide-eyed, excited, and emotional as all get-out. Already I was lonesome for my kids, but I had to swallow my guilty feelings for a while. With "Honky Tonk Girl" on the charts, I knew I had one shot at making it in the music business. We'd come too far to throw that away.

It was dark when we rolled into town. I was asleep in the backseat. When I woke up, I was all alone. It was late September, nice and cool. After calling for Doolittle, I looked around. I thought I was dreaming. Right in front of me was the Ryman Auditorium, home to the Grand Ole Opry! I couldn't get that dang car door open fast enough. I jumped out barefooted, crying happy tears. Then here come Doo, walkin' up the sidewalk. He'd got us some hot coffee and doughnuts while I was sleepin'. He said, "Hell, Loretta! What's wrong with you, standing out here, carrying on in your bare feet?" I said, "Doo, we made it! We made it to the Opry!" Doolittle always knew how to reel me in. He said, "If anyone sees you out here like this, they'll think you're crazy as hell and never let us in!" I dove back into that car headfirst.

Our next stop was a gas station bathroom to wash up. I wanted to look my best. I put on my stage outfit and freshened up. From there we went straight to the Wil-Helm Talent Agency, a large office right on Music Row in Nashville, Tennessee. The whole company was family run. Lester and Leslie, Doyle and Teddy's other brothers, were great musicians, too, and played in their band. They also worked as the booking agent and business managers, booking shows and negotiating contracts and payments, handling the money, paying bills—that type of thing.

I guess we should have called first. I had wrote them boys a letter when we left Washington, letting them know we were making our way to Nashville. They didn't think we'd just show up out of nowhere. But we did! Needless to say, they were surprised. But they fed us and took us right in, even helped us find a place to stay for a few nights.

Jumping Right In

When I put my mind to something, I'm all energy. Ask anybody. It don't matter whether I'm working in my garden, writing a song, cleaning my house, canning vegetables, or performing on the road. I've always been that way.

So I jumped into working with the Wilburn brothers like I do everything else, doing whatever it took to make a career for myself in the country music business. It felt good to have these successful musicians respect me. Artists can be insecure—we can get to thinking we're not good enough real fast. The Wilburns made me feel I belonged in Nashville. And Teddy really loved my songwriting. He said I had something different to say as a female singer/songwriter. Doyle said I could even be a bigger star than Kitty Wells. I figured that wasn't true. No one would ever be better than Kitty Wells in my eyes. But Teddy and Doyle believed I had what it took to be a great singer/songwriter, so I believed it, too. When you start really believing you can make your dreams come true, you can do about anything.

The Ernest Tubb Record Shop was right off of Broadway across from the Ryman. WSMV broadcast the Opry show, then switched straight over to broadcasting Ernest Tubb's *Midnite Jamboree*. So when the Opry let out, folks could walk on over to the Record Shop and watch the live show right there. Teddy and Doyle booked me because they had a spot for new talent. I'd be performing off-air, meaning not on the radio. But I didn't care, I just wanted to perform. And I was over the moon hoping to meet Ernest Tubb. He was my favorite male country singer. I tried to meter my songs and word rhythms like him when I wrote. My first song, "Whispering Sea," could have been his.

I'll never forget that night. It was late. There was maybe fifty people left in the building. I got up onstage, just me and my guitar. Doolittle stood by the door with Doyle. All them folks were looking at me like "Who the heck is this cowgirl?" I fastened the guitar strap on and said into the microphone, "Hello, everybody. My name is Loretta—" Before I could get out the "Lynn," those speakers let out a loud screech. It like to bust my eardrums! Everyone covered their ears. I said, "That ought to get your attention. Just hope y'all can hear me after that." Everyone laughed and I started over again. "Hello again, everybody," I said. "My name is Loretta Lynn, and tonight I'm gonna sing y'all a song I wrote. I hope ya like it."

I guess that loudspeaker squeal was a good thing, because Ernest Tubb himself was downstairs when he heard the noise. He came up to see what the heck was going on. He stood there and listened to me sing. After I came offstage, Doo and Doyle walked over. Doyle introduced us. Ernest said, "Doyle, you really have got a great up-and-coming girl singer right here." He was talking about me! I just stood there a-smilin'. I couldn't believe I was talking with the man that we'd listened to on a little transistor radio my daddy had when I was growing up. Lord, I hoped my daddy was watching from heaven. Doyle was grinning ear to ear, as usual. Ernest asked what me and Doo's plans was in Nashville. Doo never was one to mince words. He'd just say whatever, plain as day. "Well, Ernest," he said. "Our plan is for Loretta to play the Grand Ole Opry just as soon as she can." Ernest nodded and said, "Well, that's a nice plan." Doo didn't stop there. He said, "That song you just heard is already number fourteen on the country charts—and that ain't even her best one! Man, she's written hundreds!" I think Ernest liked that I wrote, too, like him. He said he'd love to hear more. I was on cloud nine.

The next day, Teddy called me into his office at Sure-Fire Music, one of the Wilburns' enterprises. He and Doyle were sitting down—Teddy behind his desk and Doyle in a chair. I sat down, too. I remember I didn't know what to do with my hands. I kept crossing and uncrossing my feet. Teddy started out telling me how much they liked me and what a talent they felt I was. They told me the Nashville music scene was hard to break into. You really had to know people. And that's still true. Nashville still has that buddy way of doing business to this day. Teddy said, "Loretta, there's a hundred great girl singers just waiting to be discovered right outside that door. But we pick you. We believe we can make something great happen for you in this business. We would like to sign you to the Wil-Helm Agency." They handed me half a dozen sheets of paper that looked like a contract. They told me to go back and talk it over with Doolittle, but they needed me to sign those papers right away. I asked why, and they said, "We may have you a spot to play the Grand Ole Opry!" What the heck! The Opry? I jumped out of that chair so fast. I jumped up and down hollerin', "Yes! Yes!" I couldn't believe my luck. Turned out Ernest Tubb had offered one of his spots on the Opry so I could play. And, friends, no one gives up their Opry spot, ever. That was Ernest for you. He was about as generous as you can be.

Doo and I signed that artist contract for the Wilburns that same day. 'Course I was still under contract with Zero Records. Doolittle told the boys what Mr. Burley said about letting us out of our recording contract, so Doyle called Mr. Burley. Mr. Burley was true to his word and released me, God bless him for that.

One week later I played the Opry for the very first time. It was one of the greatest nights of my life. Even so, I was a nervous wreck. I trembled so bad the fringe of my cowgirl dress shook. I could barely keep hold of my guitar. I stood there on the side, waiting my turn, scared to death. That big ole stage seemed endless, and I was standing there all alone. Doo had went next door to get a drink, as usual. Ernest Tubb introduced me, then somebody musta pushed me, 'cause I don't remember stepping out into the lights. All I remember is tapping my foot to the beat while

I sang "I'm a Honky Tonk Girl." I kept saying to myself, *Just don't fall down.* My legs were shaking so bad!

I'd never sang for so many people. The applause made me feel so good! Then Grant Turner, the "Voice of the Grand Ole Opry," told everybody I'd been voted Most Promising Girl Singer by the country DJs. I came offstage hollerin', "I sung on the Grand Ole Opry! I sung on the Grand Ole Opry!" Folks probably thought I was nuts. I was just happy. I couldn't believe it. Then Ott Devine, the Opry manager, asked me to come back the following week and I said yes, of course I would.

That was October 15, 1960, at the Ryman Auditorium. These days the Opry plays at the Grand Ole Opry House, a place they built for it east of Nashville. Back then it was downtown Nashville on Broadway in a building that used to be a church. Ain't nothing like the Ryman in the whole world. Good Lord, the music sounds good in there! The acoustics are amazing. The stage is round, and there's this beautiful curved balcony. And the seats are polished wooden pews. I tell you what, it feels sacred somehow. Maybe that's why folks got to callin' it the Mother Church. That was some kinda rowdy church! They packed people in. It was hot and loud with all kinds of laughing and carrying on. I loved it.

I got paid fifteen dollars for performing. I was happy to have it. We were so poor. Here I was with a hit song and we didn't have money for a motel. That goes to show you something about the business back then.

After I'd played the Opry one or two times, Doyle and

Teddy said I needed a major label behind me. So we got to work cutting demos of those six songs they'd sent.

Working with the Wilburns in the studio was a whole new world. I'd only been in a studio the one time, when Doo and I went to LA to cut those songs with Speedy West. Recording isn't like performing. To tell the truth, I hated it at first. I couldn't feel the song like when I'm telling the story to a crowd, pouring out all I have. Teddy'd say, "Okay, Loretta, let's do it again—with more feeling." He seemed disappointed I wasn't knocking the songs out of the park. He wouldn't give up on me, though. He coached me, teaching me different ways to phrase a line. He taught me timing, too. I'd been awful bad at singing before the beat before Teddy. I'd rush every line. He just wore me out until I was so dadgum tired of singing I'd slow down and get in time. Sometimes Doyle would be there. Doyle always had a smile on his face, no matter what. When Doyle was around, I'd ask him in so I'd have somebody to sing to. Doyle would sit right in front of me and I'd pretend I was singing just to him. It wouldn't matter if it was a tear-jerking song or what. Doyle always just smiled. It took about a month or so before they were happy with a few of them demos. Finally they believed they had something worth playing for the major record producers.

Doyle and Teddy's first call was to Owen Bradley, a songwriter and music arranger who'd become the best producer there was in country music. He'd produced Ernest Tubb, Kitty Wells, Chet Atkins, Brenda Lee,

Conway Twitty, and even Patsy Cline. He produced country artists for the Decca label and had a reputation for being a star-maker.

The Wilburns took Owen a demo of me singing a Sure-Fire song called "Fool #1." He liked it so much he said he wanted it for Brenda Lee to record. The Wilburns told him he could have it, but only if he signed me to the Decca label! Owen said I sounded like Kitty Wells and he already had Kitty. But Doyle said, "Owen, I'm not pitching you a song. I'm pitching you this singer." Owen agreed to give me a six-month contract and got that song for Brenda Lee to record. She did and it was a number one hit! I think that deal worked out good for me, too.

People said he was the best producer around. I really lucked out with Owen. He signed me to Decca in 1961 and that same year he was the disc jockeys' Country Man of the Year. We worked together for a lot of years—eighteen or so. We had nearly fifty hits. When I read somewhere that Owen called me the "the female Hank Williams," you could have knocked me over with a feather. I feel like that was the highest compliment I could get. Especially coming from Owen, it meant the world to me.

But back then I was just one of a handful of other new singers trying to make it in country music. It never occurred to me that I could become famous. I just wanted to make enough money to feed our family and stay in the game.

That's Show Business

The Wilburn Brothers toured the U.S. in country music package shows. This was before country music acts toured much. When you were in a package there'd be four or five different acts on one bill. Whenever they could, the boys would add me to the bill, too. So instead of Doo trying to book me in little bars and taverns all by myself, I could go with the package and sing in with them.

If you wanted to sell your records, you had to perform live. There wasn't many places to play live music in Nashville back then, if you can believe that. Nowadays you can't swing a cat and miss a live band playin' in Nashville. But then, if you wanted to get to the country music audience, you had to go to 'em. It didn't pay much, but it was something. I bet I hit every tavern in Texas. Sung right on the bar when there weren't no stages. After I got to be an Opry member, I'd tour with other acts. We'd do larger venues, like fairs and concert halls, in our package tours.

Country acts mostly did package shows. There'd be maybe a honky-tonk band, a bluegrass band, a comedian, and one woman singer. If you wanted your records on jukeboxes and the radio, that's how you did it. People had to lay eyes on you. If you were lucky, folks would call in and request your songs on the radio. Make them rise up on the charts. That helped the music sell.

I was always a big fan of radio. I'd met a lot of DJs and I stayed in touch with 'em. I'd always try to listen to WSM when I was on the road. One thing I'd do—and this was my little trick—I'd call in to request my own records. Ralph Emery was a disc jockey over there. I'd disguise my voice when I'd call. I'd say, "Hi! I'm calling from Kentucky and I wanna hear 'Success' by Loretta Lynn!" Then when we drove into a new state, I'd call up again and say, "Hey, I'm calling from Indiana. Will you play 'Success'?" I'd pretend to be somebody different every time I called. I don't think he ever did catch on. I'd do near anything to get my records played.

But every now and then someone would ask me to play a show the Wilburns didn't book. I needed the money, so if there was any way to get there, I'd take it. One time I got a call asking me to play a show in some town in Georgia. It was just a little place, but they promised to pay me seventy-five dollars. That was more than I was used to making, so of course I said yes. Doo and me got my brother Jay Lee, and we piled into our old car and Doo drove us all day to make that show. The seventy-five dollars would be enough for gas for the trip home and then a small profit. We couldn't afford a motel, but we planned to drive all night to get home.

Doo stopped at a gas station for me to change into my little stage dress, which was nothing new to me, but it tells you how tiny this tavern was—weren't no place there for me to change. It was a dumpy little place. We should've known when we saw it this wasn't goin' to turn out good. Doo went around and found the guy from the bar that called to book us. I tell you what. He looked rougher than any bar. Well, I went on and did a two-hour show—just me and Jay Lee. I didn't have a lot of songs of my own that people would know yet, so I sang every Kitty Wells and Patsy Cline song I knew, plus some Hank Williams and Ernest Tubb songs. If I knew it, we sung it. We had that place a-going. Everyone was having a great time.

After the show, Jay Lee started packing up his guitar so I went looking for Doo. Usually, I could find him by the bar with a beer, but he wasn't there. Instead, I found him outside by the back door, madder'n I had ever seen him. He was talking so fast I couldn't understand what he was so riled about. All I heard was "crook" and a lot of bad words. But then I figured it out. That scary guy we'd met behind the bar, the "SOB," as Doo called him, took off and didn't pay us. Worse, we had no money and didn't have enough gas to get back to Nashville. Well, I took a deep breath and walked back in. I told Jay Lee what was going on. I told him to unpack the guitar. I turned around and said, "Folks, we're gonna do a couple more songs." I told the whole place what happened and that we didn't have the money to get home. Those folks were so nice.

They passed a hat around and collected about twenty-five dollars for us. I was real grateful.

When Doo saw that the Wilburns were gonna fight for me like he'd been doing but they had the experience and the staff to do it, he stepped back some and let them manage my career. I still didn't make a decision without him, and he would tour with me some, but mostly it was me out there trying to make it.

He got a job as a mechanic working on big equipment like bulldozers and tractors. When folks said, "Mooney here's an auto mechanic," he'd get all hot under the collar. I guess it's all about the size of the machine.

With Doo working steady, we finally had enough money to rent a house. We found a place in Madison, just North of Nashville. It wasn't fancy—just a small brick house. But it was the nicest we'd ever lived in, either me or Doo. We'd never had a home with a bathroom before. The Wilburns gave us a housewarming party, and some of their friends chipped in to donate appliances and stuff. Rent was a hundred dollars a month. We wondered how in the hell we'd pay for it. But once we had the place, we finally felt we had our heads above the water. We could bring the kids to Nashville, and that was all I cared about.

I about had a fit when I found out that rental house was just a few blocks from where Kitty Wells and her husband, Johnny Wright, lived. The first single I ever owned was her "It Wasn't God Who Made Honky Tonk Angels," which was an answer to Hank Thompson's "The Wild Side of Life." I can't imagine I'd be where I am without Kitty. Kitty was a woman in a man's world, that's for sure, but her husband, Johnny, was her manager, and he didn't listen when Roy Acuff said that you can't make a woman the headliner in a music show. He gave Kitty the top billing in their package shows and they'd sold out. She was country music DJs' favorite female vocalist for a lot of years until Patsy Cline came along.

When Owen said I sounded like Kitty, for me that was a compliment. I'd been trying to sound like her! So it was a thrill to be living close to her. It also says something about what amounted to country music success in those days—a star living near a dirt-poor wannabe like me.

I got to meet Kitty for the first time when I was on the Opry the second or third time. I tell you, I was starstruck. My song might've been a hit single on the radio, but I was still a housewife with four kids, wearing homemade clothes, trying to catch a break. So that night me and Kitty was standing there together on the side of the stage there at the Ryman. Somebody—I don't recall who—seein' how nervous I was, said some snide remark to me, like "You'll never make it." Kitty piped up and said, real kind, "She'll do all right." I couldn't believe it! Kitty Wells, star of the Opry, was on my side! Sometimes I still hear Kitty's words in my head, "She'll do all right." If Kitty Wells was treating me like I was somebody, well, maybe I was.

Later, I got to record with Kitty. We got a Grammy nomination for "The Honky Tonk Angels Medley" that we did with k.d. lang and Brenda Lee. I'm real proud of that.

Kitty's kindness to me meant a lot. It made me start to

believe maybe I could make it in the music business. That's why I love seeing women be good friends to each other. But they tell me women make up only sixteen percent of the country artists today. And can you believe only twelve percent of the country songwriters are female? That just ain't right.

If women would stand beside each other, rather than be jealous, it'd help a lot. Like Kitty did for me. She didn't have to say much. Just, "She'll do all right." And I did.

Officially a Country Music Songwriter

After our kids came to live with us and we got settled, me and Teddy got to work writing songs for their company Sure-Fire Music. I'd never written with anyone before. That was strange at first, but before long we were writing song after song.

There were a lot of different writers at Sure-Fire. When Teddy and I weren't writing together, we'd work on songs for me to sing that another one of the Sure-Fire writers had turned in. I never asked for credit—I just wanted whatever I was singing to suit me, and I would change things around so it would. I learned a lot doing that.

I was already a recording artist with Sure-Fire signed to the Decca label, so I was surprised when the Wilburns offered me a publishing agreement, too. It's true there were already a few great country music writers who were women—Cindy Walker, Betty Sue Perry, Liz Anderson—but there weren't a lot of women writers who performed as artists, too.

Handing my songs over to be recorded by somebody

else didn't sit well with me. I was writing about my life, not somebody else's, and it was hard to imagine my songs coming out of somebody else's mouth. Plus I'd heard publishing companies like Sure-Fire got bought and sold all the time. The thought of the boys handing over the rights to what I'd wrote bothered me. I talked to Doo about it. He said, "If you don't want to sign that publishing deal, don't." But I was afraid the boys wouldn't try as hard to help me if I didn't sign it. Doo was smart. He said, "Well, put it in the contract that you'll stay with the Wilburns but they cain't sell your songs to nobody else." That was a good idea and that's what we did. The boys had no problem with adding that. So I signed my first publishing agreement with Sure-Fire Music.

It wasn't long before I was writing my songs, recording with Owen, playing the Opry, and going all around the country, singing.

I was working around the clock, working myself silly. I'd write over at Sure-Fire, record demos with Teddy, perform on the road with the Wilburns and on my own, and perform on the Opry show just as much as I could. It was exciting, but it was also a lonely time for me. Sometimes I got to feelin' mighty homesick. I didn't have no girlfriends. Back in Washington state I'd been on my own an awful lot when Doo would go doing God knows what, leaving me behind for days at a time. Now I was hardly ever alone. But I felt like I never fit in.

It took a terrible accident for my lonesome feelings to come to an end.

The Accident

When me and Doo moved to Madison in the fall of 1960, Patsy Cline was already a country music star. Fact is, me and Doo were sleeping in our car about the time Patsy and her husband, Charlie Dick, were buying their first house in Nashville, on Hillhurst Drive. That's how different our lives were! I had just the one record out with Zero, which, truth be told, wasn't much of a label at all. Patsy had changed labels and was with Decca Records, where the Wilburns had just talked Owen into signing me.

Owen Bradley was Patsy's producer and he'd convinced her to record "I Fall to Pieces." She didn't want to at first, but it's such a great fit for her voice, so rich and smooth. Listening to Patsy sing "I Fall to Pieces" about made me cry my eyes out. It was like Patsy felt what I felt, deep down. Before that, songs about cheating were real popular. This was different. When Patsy sang it, her way of singing made you believe every single word. It was like she was singing about something she'd been through. You can hear every bit of pain and longing in her voice. There's even a catch in her voice if you listen close. She didn't just sing the words. She felt 'em.

It's a tough song to sing, too—and she recorded it when she was seven months pregnant. If you've ever tried to sing it, you know what I mean when I say that was something! It takes a lot of deep breathing. About a week after Little Randy was born on January 21, 1961, Decca released "I Fall to Pieces." It didn't get much radio play until around March.

Her single hadn't been out long when, on Wednesday, June 14, 1961, Patsy and her brother were in a terrible car accident. They'd been shopping over in Madison. Patsy'd bought some fabric for her momma to make her some dresses. Sam was driving them home in the rain.

A car coming the other way gunned it, tryin' to pass another car on a double yellow line. That lady driver hit Patsy's car head-on on a part of Old Hickory Boulevard that wraps all around Nashville. Poor Patsy got thrown against the windshield and her head broke through.

News of the wreck was on the radio. Dottie West, another singer-songwriter who was having some really good success of her own, heard it and drove straight over to the site of the accident with curlers in her hair. Patsy'd insisted that the medics see to her brother and the folks in the other car first, so she was there on the side of the road, bleeding. She'd cut an artery and there was lots of blood. Dottie stayed with Patsy and rode with her in the ambulance, picking glass out of her hair as they sped to the hospital. She was admitted as "critical." Two of the folks in the other car died. It was awful.

It's a wonder Patsy made it. The doctor, Dr. Hillis Evans, told Charlie her injuries were life-threatening. Charlie sat up worrying all night while they operated on her for hours. The doctor told Charlie her injuries were so serious that it looked hopeless. She was a mess. A broken and dislocated hip, a bad cut on her right arm, and her face was cut up awful. She was in real bad shape and it seemed like everyone in Nashville was pulling for her. I didn't know it at the time, but a bunch of folks from the Opry gathered outside Madison Hospital during surgery and kept watch all night. That same night, Patsy called for Charlie and said, "Jesus was here, Charlie. Don't worry. He took my hand and told me, 'No, not now. I have other things for you to do.'"

Then on Friday, Charlie told reporters Patsy was off the critical list and her doctor said her condition was "fair." Telegrams, cards, letters, and flowers came pouring in over at the hospital for her. The operators at the phones said emergency callers weren't able to get through 'cause of all the phone calls for Patsy. It got to where they couldn't handle it all. Charlie had to tell reporters that folks needed to stop calling the hospital. Patsy's brother was already sitting up and in a wheelchair, but Patsy was still bad off. She couldn't have any visitors except family.

Here You Are!

I was playin' the Opry show one hot night in July when Grant Turner updated the audience about Patsy's condition and asked for prayers. I was just tore up about poor Patsy. She'd had a special place in my heart ever since I saw her on Arthur Godfrey. After the show ended we walked over to the Record Shop and Doo asked Ernest if I could sing. He said I sure could. Ernest and me got to talkin' about Patsy's wreck. Like I said, I was pretty tore up. He said, "Now, Loretta, honey, don't you cry. Patsy's hanging on. She's a trouper." I don't know if he'd seen her or what. But I told him I had an idea. He listened and he agreed.

When it was my turn, instead of singing my own song, I said, "Friends, I'd like to do something special for someone I admire a great deal. This is the hit song by Miss Patsy Cline that's way up there on the charts. I guess y'all know she's over there in Madison in the hospital 'cause she's been in a real bad car wreck. So I want to dedicate this to her. Patsy, if you're a-listenin', honey, this song's for you. 'I Fall to Pieces.' I hope you get well real soon." I didn't know the words right yet, so Doo held up a copy of *Country Song Roundup* for me to read while I played my guitar.

Patsy's husband, Charlie Dick, had snuck a radio into the hospital, so him and Patsy were up listening to the Opry show and then the *Midnite Jamboree*, too. Well, they heard me sing. Patsy sent Charlie right over. He found me and said, "Are you Loretta Lynn?" I said, "Yes, sir!" But I didn't know who he was—just a handsome man. He introduced himself and I was just as happy as I could be. I threw my arms around him and squeezed him tight. I told him it was a big thrill for me to meet Patsy Cline's husband. Then he surprised me. He said, "Patsy wants to see you. She wants me to bring you to the hospital." Well, I was so happy and confused. I didn't know what to think. I like to had a fit. We couldn't go that night—it was way past visiting hours. But the next day Doo drove me out to the hospital.

Maybe I should've been scared, going to talk to Patsy Cline. I'd just sung one of her best-known songs and probably botched it. But I wasn't scared. I was thrilled. I was cocky, sure of myself, sure I was just as good as any other woman—or man, for that matter—singing in those days. My mama used to say, "Never let people think you're not worth something." I'd played at the Grand Ole Opry, hadn't I? I was no slouch. I couldn't wait to meet Patsy Cline.

So I went up to Patsy's room on the fourth floor. Charlie took me in to see her. There were flowers everywhere. The room was bright and cheery, but I could see right away that Patsy was banged up bad. Her leg must've been broke, because it was in a cast and wired up to the ceiling. Her head was bandaged all the way up into her hair. She was in pain, but when I followed Charlie in, she said, "Here you are!" Real nice. It was like she'd been waitin' to see me. I said, "Hello, Patsy. I'm Loretta Lynn." She thanked me for singing her song and I thanked her for inviting me. I was feeling so many things at once—happy to be meeting her and also so sad that she was hurt.

She told me to sit down, so I did. She said, "I finally did it! 'I Fall to Pieces' hit number one! Ain't that incredible!" She grabbed my hand. "I never want to record again," she said. "I just want to enjoy this one song forever." Patsy could be dramatic.

We talked about me being new to Nashville. She said I was a real good singer—that I had all the other girls running scared. She laughed, though, so I knew she didn't mean her. Patsy Cline wasn't afraid of nobody! We traded stories about what all goes on at the Opry and in the entertainment business. And we laughed a lot. It was like we knew each other already. It's funny how we just started talking that way, 'cause I was real shy. Patsy never was shy.

'Course we had a lot in common. We were the same age. We both grew up poor. Both of us had to grow up too fast. Neither one of us went to high school. She went to work to help support her family. Me? I married the first boy I ever kissed, followin' him halfway across the country, having babies when I wasn't more than a girl myself.

But I was new to the music business and Patsy wasn't. She'd been performing real regular for twelve years. She'd moved to Nashville a couple of years before to pursue her big dreams. Now here she was holed up in a hospital while her song was a number one country single! Randy was having to cancel her shows left and right when they should've been bookin' more. Patsy said it took six nurses to keep her in that bed!

I'd barely gotten to Nashville. I had so much to learn. But somehow Patsy still treated me like an equal. Maybe she saw herself in me and was rooting for me like she was rooting for herself? I don't know.

Patsy asked me about the Wilburns. She'd had some bad experiences with management and contracts. When it came to somebody being in control of her career, she was real wary. I was glad when she said she'd heard good things about the boys. I had never talked to anyone besides Doo about the Wilburns. Patsy said she liked their singing, too. They'd been singing since they were kids, just like us. I remember she said with a big laugh, "That Teddy Wilburn is a looker, too." Teddy and Doyle both were handsome men, for sure, but all the women seemed to like Teddy the best, even Patsy.

Patsy listened to music all the time. Even in the hospital she had a radio going twenty-four hours a day. Not me. I'd listen in the car with Doo or every now and then at the house. But I'd figured out that listening to the radio messed with my songwriting. I'd hear something that was maybe a tad close to some song I'd started, or maybe in the same line of an idea, and it would stop me from finishing that song.

Patsy confessed her darkest fear: What if her music career was over after what she'd been through? She said her face was busted up so bad, there was no tellin' how long it'd take to recover. Image matters a lot in the entertainment business, she said. But I encouraged Patsy. I told her everything was gonna be all right. I really felt like the best was yet to come for her.

What else did we talk about that day? Everything and nothing. Clothes. She'd always liked fashion. She designed a lot of her own clothes that her momma sewed for her. She laughed, telling me about an ugly skirt she'd made. 'Course there was girl talk about our husbands, once Charlie and Doo left the room. Those boys gave us plenty to talk about.

Let's get something straight right here. In the movie of *Coal Miner's Daughter* they made it look like Charlie snuck beer into the hospital. I don't believe it. That hospital was real religious. The Seventh Day Adventists ran it, and they wouldn't even let Patsy eat meat in there! Now, Charlie mighta snuck in some home-cooking from Patsy's momma. I can see that. But that would've been hard to show in a movie. Maybe that's why they showed beer.

Did I know meeting Patsy that day would change my life? No. How could I? But I knew I'd found a real friend: a great singer, a proud momma, a woman who wasn't afraid to stand up for herself. Another woman with music burning in her blood.

Before we left, Patsy asked Doo and I to come over for dinner once she got out of that hospital. There was no way I would've said no. From that day on, me and Patsy was friends.

Destined to Be a Star

Patsy was born Virginia "Ginny" Hensley, the oldest of three kids. Her daddy, Sam Hensley, was quite a bit older than her momma, Hilda Patterson, and a mean drunk. Hilda worked her fingers to the bone keeping their family afloat while Sam lived high on the hog, with no way to pay for it. They moved nineteen times, so Patsy didn't get to stay in one school long or keep friends. The only constant in her life was music. Even as a little kid she played piano by ear. Both her momma and daddy loved music, too.

Patsy told me things about her childhood—things I promised to take to my grave. I'll say this and that's all: By the time she was eleven she'd lived a woman's life. It hurt her a lot. She said, "He made me grow up before my time." Me and Patsy understood each other. I hadn't been through what Patsy had, but I understood. Hell, when I was fifteen, I felt like I was thirty. Then when I got to be thirty, it was like I was still fifteen.

Sam Hensley left the family when Patsy was sixteen. He

left her and her momma, her little brother and sister in Winchester, Virginia, in a house on the wrong side of the railroad tracks. From then on, Patsy and Hilda raised each other. Hilda was Patsy's closest friend. She was a seamstress, she took in laundry, was a waitress, did whatever she had to. They never had much, but they were close.

Patsy quit school to help pay the bills. Her first job was slitting chicken throats at a meat packing plant, but they fired her when they found out she was too young. Then she worked as the counter girl at the Greyhound bus station. She settled for a while serving sodas at Gaunt's Drug Store. She'd sing on the radio and perform whenever she could with local bands. She told folks, "I'm going to be something one of these days. I won't be a waitress for the rest of my life." She was a big dreamer and she set her heart on making it as a singer somehow, someway. Like me, she wanted to take care of her family.

Hilda was Patsy's biggest fan. She made all her colorful costumes. She even took Patsy to Nashville to audition for the Grand Ole Opry when she was just seventeen. That sounds young to me—until I remember I had two babies by then. So I guess it's all in how you look at it. Even though Patsy didn't get on back then because of the age restrictions, she got to meet a lot of country music folks who encouraged her, including Roy Acuff, the King of Country Music at the time. He overheard her auditioning and invited her to sing on his *Dinner Bell* broadcast later that day. That inspired her to keep plugging away.

Patsy, still known then as "Ginny," went back home

and sang wherever she could—radio shows, church socials, benefits, fraternal parties, carnivals. She sang pretty regular with a local band at Rainbow Inn. When she auditioned for Bill Peer and the Melody Boys and Girls, Bill fell for her right away—and who can blame him? He believed she was going to be a big star. Him and Patsy played in hotels and taverns and honky-tonks. She wasn't just singing locally anymore. She was traveling everywhere.

Patsy quit that drugstore job on her twentieth birthday to sing full time. Bill was calling himself her manager. Truth is, Bill was in love with her. He swore he was gonna make Patsy a star. Bill's claim to fame might be that he's the one who gave her the stage name Patsy, short for her middle name, "Patterson."

When she married Gerald Cline she became "Patsy Cline." Gerald was eight years older and already divorced twice. Their marriage didn't last long. Gerald knew Patsy was a lead singer, but somehow he wanted Patsy waiting for him when he came home from work. Her divorce was finalized when she was twenty-three, right around the time she got a recording contract with 4 Star Records. It's funny because her first single was "A Church, a Courtroom, and Then Goodbye," a song about getting a divorce. When she sung that song you could tell she lived it. Turned out that deal with 4 Star was a mess. They only let Patsy record songs their songwriters wrote and the pickin's were slim. It took her a long time to get out that deal.

Her big break was *Arthur Godfrey's Talent Scouts*—the TV show where I saw her back in Washington state. It was one of the most popular shows at the time. Patsy got to be a regular on that show. Once 4 Star released the single for "Walkin' After Midnight" it stayed on the charts—both country and pop. That's when Patsy started touring and making appearances on the live country music circuit based out of Nashville.

Just a few days before that famous TV performance, Patsy married Charlie Dick, who she'd met when she was singing in clubs back in Virginia. Charlie was a ladies' man, but he was crazy about Patsy. He'd been courting her for years. They were wild for each other. Randy Hughes was her manager by then. Randy was the one who convinced her to make the move to Nashville. That was two years before we met.

Patsy could do anything with that voice. Randy wanted to highlight the sensual part with torch songs. That was different from anything else in country music. Patsy liked that idea. It was Owen Bradley who really brought out Patsy's musical best. He was the greatest A&R man that I've ever known or ever will know. He signed Patsy to the Decca label when she finally got out from under her contract with 4 Star Records. Owen had such a good ear. I mean his ear was sharp. People don't know he was also an amazing pianist, and a great arranger. If Owen arranged it, it was good. He made slick-sounding records. He might bring in strings, horns, drums, the works.

Patsy considered herself a country singer, even once her country hits crossed over to the pop charts. Me? I was country as cornbread. Patsy was more versatile. She had perfect pitch. I mean it: Patsy could tell you a note just by hearing it once. It's hard to imagine what Patsy's career would have been without Owen. He famously told her, "You're one of the meanest bitches I've ever met." She just laughed. She loved it. After that they were able to be peers. I guess it opened them up to have that kind of honesty between them. Owen pushed her and helped her grow. But there was never any question about who had the last word about what she would and wouldn't do. That was always Patsy.

They Work for You

I was with Patsy at her house when she was talking on the phone with Randy, her manager. She was itching to get back to work and even though she wasn't out of the hospital yet, she didn't want him canceling any more shows. She was giving him an earful. She said, "I don't care what you want, Randy Hughes! You work for me. I don't work for you."

I was shocked. If my managers said, "Jump," I'd ask, "How high, boys?" I did whatever they said. They told me where to go, when to go, and how much I'd get paid. They told me what to wear. Lately they'd even been telling me how to walk. Teddy was determined to get me out of my cowgirl boots. He'd bought me some panty hose and heels and made me walk up and down the halls in the office. I was like a drunk trying to walk a straight line. I hadn't mastered it yet.

"Gosh, Patsy," I said. "How can you talk to your manager that way? I'd be scared to talk to Doyle or Teddy like that." She said, "Hells bells, Loretta! Those boys are your managers, not your bosses! They don't employ you. Listen, if you make it to the big time, they hit the jackpot. And trust me, if you don't make them money, there will be another hot new artist that comes along to take your place, and, honey, they won't even bat an eye. I've seen it," Patsy said. "A hundred times."

I didn't say anything, but I thought, *The boys aren't like that. I trust them.* But I'd remember that conversation years later when the Wilburns sued me for five million dollars. I'll tell more about that later.

Patsy had been burned plenty of times in the past. She'd been taken advantage of by her managers and music publishers, and she wasn't about to let it happen again. When I told Patsy and Charlie what happened in that Georgia tavern, Patsy said, "Loretta, you have to get at least half your money up front." She said she learned that the hard way. "No dough, no show—that's my rule," she said.

I was surprised she could get them to pay her the money before she performed. Patsy said, "Honey, we're women, so they think we have to put up with that crap." Once she said that, I realized it was true. I never heard about male artists being ripped off. Still, I told Patsy I felt bad asking for money. "Maybe I can get the boys to ask for half up front from now on," I said. Patsy said, "Come on, Loretta, get some balls!" 'Course that made me laugh. "You're gonna need them in this business. If you don't, you will starve to death."

I learned a lot watching Patsy. Nashville was always a funny place, and the rules never made much sense to me. Folks liked to keep it real polite and low-key, especially when they were talkin' business. Seemed like you were supposed to act like you didn't care about money—especially as a woman. Patsy was clear about what she wanted. She knew how to get it, too.

The Cline's Doin' Just Fine

The hospital released Patsy late that July, all bandaged up and in a wheelchair. She was still in pain, but she desperately wanted her fans and everybody to know she was okay. Plus, she was itching to get back to work. Since "I Fall to Pieces" was at the top of the charts, Randy could book her for gigs that'd pay better than ever. Nothin' and nobody was gonna keep her down.

So on July 22, 1961, just days after leaving the hospital, she was back at the Grand Ole Opry. As Charlie wheeled Patsy onstage, the crowd gave her a standing ovation! She couldn't sing, of course, but somebody lowered the mike for her to talk. She got emotional as she thanked everyone. She said, "At the very time when I needed you the most, you came through with the flying-est of colors. You'll never know how happy you made this ole country gal." She promised to be back soon to sing her new hit song.

It was real important to Patsy how much her fans loved her. All those letters and flowers and the outpouring of support fortified her. When she was with her fans, performing or signing autographs or talking to reporters, she'd drink in their love and it made her stronger. She glowed. Her fans gave her so much love and affection. She'd stay until the last person had left who wanted her autograph or wanted to take her picture. That's how much she loved it.

As happy as Patsy was to be back onstage to greet her fans, she needed to perform. "I've got to get back to work," she said. "I can't stand this another minute!" Her hospital stay was the longest she'd ever gone without performing.

Patsy was booked before her accident to sing at the Cimarron Ballroom in Tulsa, Oklahoma. Her doctor didn't want her to go, but she went anyway. That was Patsy. If she wanted to do something, nobody could stop her. She said, "What them doctors don't know won't hurt 'em." In Tulsa, she showed up on crutches and sat on a stool to perform. Decca/MCA recorded the performance. They released the recording in 1997. If you listen, you can hear Patsy talkin' about the accident and how glad she was to be back. She sings her hit, "I Fall to Pieces," and some of her other favorites. When I hear her sing "Lovesick Blues" on that recording, I can't believe she could yodel so good after all her poor body'd went through! Cracked ribs and all.

Hello, Little Gal

Once Patsy was back at home, she and Charlie invited us over for dinner, just like she'd promised. We drove up to their little brick house on Hillhurst Drive. When we got there, Patsy said, "Hello, Little Gal!" like we'd known each other our whole lives. Most folks were "Hoss" to Patsy, but she called me Little Gal from the start. I'd borrowed a gray skirt from my sister-in-law, and I felt right plain next to Patsy. She wore a pretty little apron over her dress, hobbling around her kitchen with a crutch, getting along pretty good. She was on them crutches for a good bit after the accident.

She was a great hostess. Here she was, this big music star, and she didn't have nobody helping her. She had music playing and Charlie was bartender. They made us feel right welcome.

Dinner was as fancy as you could get in those days: broiled shrimp and mashed potatoes. Seemed to me Patsy went to a lot of effort to make a nice dinner for me and Doo when we weren't nobody. We hadn't been treated all that good when we got to town and here Patsy Cline was rollin' out this nice meal. It didn't feel *too* fancy, though, the way Patsy made it. It was just real good. She was a great cook.

I noticed differences, eating at Patsy's. The way I was brought up, we were lucky to use a fork, never mind a knife. Patsy didn't come from much, either, but she ate like the Queen of England. She'd turn the fork over upside down, push the food onto it with her knife. I watched her, real careful, to see how she done it. Some folks with good manners will try and make you feel small, showin' off with 'em. Patsy was never like that. She was just enjoying herself and making us feel welcome.

Seemed to me that Patsy Cline was even more glamorous and fun in person than she was when she was performing. She cracked a lot of jokes. She liked to see what she could get away with as far as jokes go. Me? I cracked jokes right back at her. From the earliest days, we were like old friends meeting again. I think she got tired of always feeling like she had something to prove, trying to make it as a woman in the business. But she didn't have nothin' to prove with me. We got to be close quick.

Doo and Charlie hit it off good, too. Doo didn't take to people real easy, but those two were cut from the same cloth. If they hadn't of been, Doo might have took off before the meal was done, made some excuse. Patsy and I would've been friends anyhow, but our husbands getting along so good made me relax a little more that first night.

After the talking and laughing and the eating, Patsy

played some demos Owen had sent over. I learned that Patsy didn't write her own songs. Like Dean Martin and Frank Sinatra, she could take a song someone else wrote and make it her own. It had to be a song she could feel in her gut, then she'd sing the hell out of it.

Patsy said Owen wanted songs that would work with the teenagers. It was the teens that bought the singles, he said, and that helped drive a song up the charts. The adults bought the LP albums, but sales by teenagers made songs hit the charts.

The label was trying to get Patsy to be more of a pop singer. She told me in her heart she considered herself a country singer. When she performed, she liked upbeat, country and western songs. They were her bread and butter. Even though Patsy thought of herself that way, Owen said it didn't matter. She could be both. Owen knew how to make pop-sounding records. He'd produced both "Walkin' After Midnight" when she was with 4 Star and "I Fall to Pieces." His New York bosses wanted more of that. 'Course nobody could boss Patsy.

One of the songs she played us was called "Crazy." Patsy said she was still on the fence about whether to record it or not—and that was all Charlie's fault. See, Charlie met a songwriter at Tootsies Orchid Lounge who went by the name Hugh Nelson. This guy had written "Hello Walls" for Faron Young, which had been a hit for him. This "Hugh Nelson"—who we now know as Willie—found out Charlie was married to Patsy Cline, and he gave Charlie "Crazy."

Charlie loved it. He tried to convince Patsy to record it, but she didn't like it. In Nelson's demo he talked through the lyrics, and she didn't like the style of it. Charlie kept her up late that night, listening to that record over and over. She said he'd soured her on it. But there was something special about the song. Owen liked the song, too, and believed she should record it. After the success of "I Fall to Pieces," Patsy trusted Owen's instincts. Patsy said, "It's good, but there ain't no way I can sing it like that guy." Owen agreed—and said her version would be better. Patsy had the perfect voice for that song.

That night at Patsy's house was the first time since me and Doo came to Nashville that I felt at home.

The Henhouse Brigade and a Mini-Breakdown

I was spending a lot of time with Patsy. We'd talk on the phone and I'd go over there to help her get things done. It wasn't always just me. Dottie West was there a lot, too. And Brenda Lee and Pearl Miller. Charlie got to callin' us the "henhouse brigade." Patsy liked to be a mother hen, so the name made sense. She loved a full house. She liked all the kids running around and all kinds of music playing at all hours. She was happiest surrounded by people she loved and who loved her. I don't think she liked to be alone much, to tell the truth.

As I've said before, Patsy was a heck of a good cook. She enjoyed fixin' big meals for her friends and family and she sure knew her way around a kitchen. This was a side of Patsy a lot of people didn't get to see: Patsy at home with her family and the people she loved. She was in the spotlight so much that it's how she's remembered—as a fantastic performer with a heartbreaking voice. I feel lucky that I got to see her at-home-cooking side.

Once Patsy got to feeling better and mending from the car accident, she really started to like being at home—it was a special time for her. Putting her babies to sleep at night and waking up and making them all breakfast. The kinds of small, normal things that we all can take for granted if we're not careful. Soon Patsy was inviting ten to twenty guests over for a big meal. She'd make most of it herself. It was never anything fancy. I'd get a phone call and it would be Patsy saying, "Hey, gal. You, Mooney, and the kids come over for dinner tonight. I am making a big ham."

"That sounds great," I'd say. "I'll make some potatoes to bring."

Patsy would reply, "I already made potatoes."

"Well, some baked beans, then."

But, no matter what I could think of, she would have already made it. I'd bring a dish of something anyway, 'cause I knew she had called more friends than just Doo and me to come eat. It was hard to outcook Patsy on anything, but I have to say (and she'd tell you, too) that I could fry the best chicken! My other big dish was chicken and dumplin's—thank goodness we raised our own chickens.

Charlie and Doo had a few good times of their own over the old charcoal grill. They got pretty good at grilling meat together. We all started calling those get-togethers the "Patsy PotLucks." They were the best times.

One afternoon Charlie called me up. "Loretta?" he said and didn't wait for me to answer. Didn't even say who it was, just dove right in. That made me nervous.

"Hello, Charlie," I said. "Is Patsy okay?" I held my breath. I don't know why for sure. Something in his voice had me worried.

Charlie could be a handful, but he had been real sweet with Patsy since she got out of the hospital. She was back to work, recovering a little bit every day, but her recovery was bound to take a while. Hilda came down from Virginia to help with the kids and the house. Everyone wanted Patsy to get better. We all knew it would be a tough road to recovery.

Patsy was a strong person, and she wouldn't let anyone baby her. She didn't want any pity. She was determined to get over this hump and come back better than ever. The brave Patsy face. That is what she showed everyone around her. But Patsy was in pain. She never let it show, though. Instead, she made fun of herself, calling herself names like Patsy Crutch-Leg. She'd talk about her "new hairline." To look at her head you'd think someone took a knife and sliced her clear across the forehead and then sewed it back together. She kept it covered up so folks wouldn't stare.

That afternoon, Charlie asked me if Doolittle could drop me by their place for a visit. He said Patsy was really having a hard day. He hoped maybe I could cheer her up. I said I'd come right away. I didn't like the sound of his voice. I could tell he was just trying to hold himself together.

I had Doolittle half scared to death driving me over there, trying to make him go faster. Charlie met us at the front door. Patsy was lying down in the bedroom, he said. So I started down the hall. When I opened the door, Patsy wasn't in the bed. She was in the bathroom and she was a crying mess. She had a hair cap on her head, mascara running down her face. Makeup was scattered everywhere like she'd shoved it all onto the floor. I slowly walked in and sat down on the little square vanity seat beside her. I didn't say a word. I just wrapped my arm around her shoulder and let her cry.

When she pulled away she said, "I scared little Julie half to death today." Her daughter was around three years old at the time. I said, "Why? What do you mean?" She said, "She didn't even recognize her own momma!" Patsy told me she'd ordered a bunch of hairpieces, blonde-, red-, and brunette-colored wigs of different lengths, thinking she could wear them to cover the large scar from her hairline through her right eyebrow. That morning she'd tried covering up her scars with makeup and put on one of the wigs—just to try out the look. When little Julie saw Patsy, she took off just a-runnin'. Patsy shook her head. "All my tough talk about how I'll be back, sayin' 'Don't count me out! The Cline's doin' just fine.'" She threw her hands up in the air. "Damn it! Do I look fine? Do I look fine to you, Loretta? My own kid doesn't know me!"

Nothing I could say would change her feeling right then, I knew that. All I could do was let her talk. When she was all talked out, she looked at her reflection in the mirror. She whispered, "I wish I would wake up from this bad dream."

I got up then and started picking up all those makeup bottles and tubes throwed all over the floor. It was the only thing I could think of to do to help. She turned to me and said, "Loretta, I don't think I will ever be the same."

"You're right," I said. "You won't. The good Lord spared you for a reason, Patsy. And I am happy he did." I sat down again softly beside her. I dabbed a little cold cream on a cloth and began wiping her makeup off. I said, "I didn't know you back before that god-awful wreck. All I have to go by is who I see now. I see a brave friend, a great mother and wife, and hey, one of the greatest country singers in the whole dadgum world. I think you just gotta let go of the old Patsy to love the new one. And I think the new one is pretty great."

Patsy turned and put on a dark red wig. I said, "Heck, Patsy. Ain't no wonder you scared little Julie in that thang! You look like a porcupine." That got a smile out of her. I got a brush and went to work on that hair.

When Patsy and me came out, Doo and Charlie were working on Charlie's car. We took a seat in the lawn chairs, drinking Coca-Colas, and acted like nothin' ever happened.

That wouldn't be the last time Patsy broke down. She was a pro at putting on makeup, but she was having a hard time adjusting to her new face. Patsy'd drawn on her eyebrows for years, even before the wreck. Now she had a thick scar where her eyebrow used to be, leaving Patsy to draw in that whole right eyebrow across it. Drawing over that big scar was hard. She hadn't managed to get it just right. After she gave Julie that fright, Patsy decided to hire a professional makeup artist to help her learn to apply makeup to her new face.

Crazy

The country music community was small back then. It wasn't unusual for artists to sit in on each other's recording sessions. I'd only ever been in the studio with the Wilburns. So when Patsy invited me to come along to her first recording session since the accident, I jumped at the chance. That was August 17, 1961, barely a month after she got out of the hospital.

Owen's recording studio was a funny-looking building behind his offices on Sixteenth Avenue South. Nowadays we call that Music Row. I got to know that place real well in the years to come, but right then it was new to me. Different.

For Patsy, Owen's studio was just as comfortable as home. She walked in to warm greetings all around. 'Course her leg hadn't healed all the way, so she hobbled in on crutches. She joked about it with the guys, then propped them on the wall and leaned against a stool to sing. For harmony, Owen had brought in the Jordanaires, who backed up Elvis Presley. Patsy said, "Owen, don't let them four voices cover me up."

"Leave that to me," he said. "You'll be all right."

We used to record four or five songs in a day, but we didn't know how well Patsy'd be feeling and if she'd be up for that. Turned out she was in great form. She recorded "San Antonio Rose" and "A Poor Man's Roses (Or a Rich Man's Gold)."

Patsy liked to go fast, to keep a live audience on their toes. That's the way she'd come up in the business, singing for people who needed you to grab their attention. That "Y'all, come on in!" style worked for a lot of years. But in the studio, Owen challenged her to slow down on every song. She got so mad when he'd say, "Slow down." If you ask me, that's when she sang best—when she was mad. Her voice got thick with emotion. Listen and you can hear her take her time on "The Wayward Wind." It's so good. And her version of Cole Porter's "True Love" was beautiful. It really got me.

Seemed like Patsy was on a roll. So Owen pulled out "Crazy." His arrangement was different from Willie's. It was jazzy with a deep bass guitar and two pianos.

As soon as Patsy sang those first few notes, I knew Owen was right. Sure, they were Willie's lyrics, but it felt for all the world like it was Patsy's life. Like she was spilling her own heart out. Like she'd opened up a window into her soul.

But Patsy's ribs were still too sore. She was struggling, having a hard time with the high notes. She tried and tried again. Her lungs weren't ready. It made her so mad. And I could tell it hurt her pride.

Owen said, "No sense killing yourself. Go on home." He said, "You go rest. I'll lay down the tracks with the guys. You can come back to record the vocals when you're ready." That was pretty unusual back then, isolating a singer's voice like that, but Owen was good. He was ahead of his time.

A few days later, Patsy came back in. Owen recorded her singing "Crazy" and she did that whole song in one take. Say what you want, but I think that's just magical.

Leave It to the Professional

Patsy was in a good mood. She'd found a makeup artist to come to the house. She called me up, real hopeful. "Want to come over and watch? Maybe you can learn a thing or two," she said. I said, "Sure!" Lord knows I didn't have a clue about half of that stuff. I had Doo bring me right over, but I didn't tell him what we were up to. He didn't like me wearing makeup.

Around lunchtime, a funny-looking yellow car pulled up into Patsy's drive, going too fast. It looked like a foreign car you'd see in England or something. A little woman around four feet tall stepped out. She wasn't old—maybe forty—and I wondered for a minute if it was one of Patsy's relatives come to visit, because she was carrying two huge overnight cases. She was so tiny she could barely carry them herself.

Then Patsy said, "Oh, look, she's here!" It wasn't a relative. It was the makeup lady.

Patsy opened up the front door and shouted, "Hey, Hoss! You need some help?"

I went out and took one of those cases for this little lady. She stumbled through the door and almost fell. I thought, *This poor woman don't have a clue where she is. How's she gonna put somebody's face on?* But Patsy was too busy to notice. She was setting up cups of water for cleaning makeup sponges and stuff. So I just sat back and watched.

The lady said, "I need to be paid up front." I thought that was strange. I whispered to Patsy, "Hey, you think this old gal is okay?" Patsy said sure, sure, she was fine, and handed the woman a twenty-dollar bill, which, by the way, was a heck of a lot of money back then. I got paid less than that for my first performance at the Opry, remember? Patsy whispered, "She's from New York, Loretta. They're all this way." I said, "New York, nothing. She's drunk." Patsy laughed and told me to hush.

The woman told Patsy to sit down and lay her head back. She opened up a case and, Lord, she had all kinds of creams. She started rubbing cream on Patsy's face. Patsy just closed her eyes and smiled like she had really reached the top of the glamour scale. After what seemed like hours of this lady applying all kinds of who-knows-what on her face, Patsy raised up her head.

Holy shit, I thought. I didn't know what to say. That makeup job was so bad. Friends, I swear Patsy looked like a poorly made up drag queen. Patsy took one look at my face and marched to the bathroom to look in the mirror. I knew what was coming. I told that makeup lady, "Miss, you best be packing up your stuff." Patsy was gonna flip her top.

All of a sudden I heard, "What in the hell?" I followed Patsy back into the bathroom. She turned from the mirror and said, "I am gonna kick her ass." I said, "Oh, come on, Patsy. It's just makeup. It's not that bad." But it wasn't good, either, that was for sure. I stuck my head back out the bathroom door and hollered at the makeup lady to get goin'. I didn't know how much longer I could hold Patsy back from whooping that lady's behind. And it was all I could do not to bust out laughing at this outrageous makeup job.

Patsy stormed out of the bathroom yelling at that lady to get out, swearing she'd never get another job in Nashville. This lady was stuffing her things into those overnight cases—just throwin' stuff in. She was sobering up pretty fast. Patsy said, "I want my money back." But that crazy lady said, "No refunds," and took off out the front door. I couldn't hold back anymore. I laughed so hard. I laughed so hard that I peed myself! Patsy went back in the bathroom, but I stood there at the door, watching that makeup lady run for her car. One of her cases busted open and spilled all over the driveway. I went out and helped her pick up all the bottles and tubes of God knows what. That stuff was everywhere. I bet there's still old lipstick tubes out there in that yard.

When I got back inside, Patsy was washing her face. Whatever that woman used to draw on Patsy's eyebrows was some good stuff. I mean it didn't look good as far as how she drew them on Patsy, but that pencil took days to completely wear off.

Patsy finally decided she was her own best makeup artist. And she was. After a while, Patsy got to doing her makeup so good that even with all the scarring on her forehead she looked like a movie star. She'd ask, "How do I look? How's my brow?" And I told her the God's honest truth: "You look beautiful."

It Was Just a Razor

Patsy and I didn't sit around talking about the music business and performing all the time. We spent time together 'cause we enjoyed each other's company. And it turns out I learned a lot from her—things an older sister might've taught me, if I had one.

Most every woman in America was shaving their legs by the 1960s, but, well, honestly, folks, I never did. I ain't embarrassed about that. It wasn't like I was as hairy as a bear. Fact is, I had never had a lot of body hair at all, especially on my legs. My mommy didn't, either. Some might think it's a good thing. So I guess shaving never crossed my mind.

When I married Doolittle he didn't say anything about my legs. Not one single word to me about why I didn't shave 'em. Doo was older and had many girlfriends before (and after) me, so if me having a few hairs on my legs was a big deal, surely he would have told me. Then again, me and Doo didn't talk about things like that. The only time he talked was if he had something for me to do. And that was all the time.

I'd gotten to where I wore dresses onstage, but I still had never thought a thing about shaving my legs. I wore pedal pushers unless I was workin'. My stage dresses at that time were kind of long—right below the knee—and I wore cowgirl boots most of the time, so no one was or should have been looking at my legs anyway.

Well, one day Patsy called and invited me over. She had a few new stage outfits to show me. Fashion was a passion for Patsy, and she was so proud of those dresses. We went to her bedroom and she had all them dresses laid out on the bed. One had thousands of rhinestones all over it and they just sparkled and shined. I had never seen a dress as fancy as that. Patsy must've seen how much I liked it because she said, "Here, Little Gal, you try this on. Let's see how it looks on you."

"No, Patsy," I said. "I don't want to risk tearing up your new dress." 'Course Patsy never took no for an answer.

So there I was, sitting on the bed in just my slip, waiting for her to hand me that dress, and Patsy looked down at my legs. She hollered, "Loretta, honey! You need to shave your legs!"

I looked down, confused. I said, "Shave my legs? Why?"

I swear I thought Patsy was going to pass out from laughing, which by the way makes me so mad. I hate when people laugh at me. I stood right up. I said, "I don't know what you think is so funny, Patsy. My mommy said the Good Lord gave us all the hair on our body!" Well, that made her laugh even more.

"Loretta Lynn, don't tell me you have never shaved your legs."

I must have had a stupid look on my face. I know I was turning red. I felt so embarrassed. Patsy stopped laughing then and took my arm. Real sweet, she said, "Come on, Little Gal. I am going to show you how to have the smoothest legs in Nashville, Tennessee."

We made our way to her bathroom and she got two razors out. She mixed us up a little shaving cream, then she ran a little warm water in the tub. Both of us sat there side by side together on the edge of her tub as it filled. Patsy walked me through shaving my legs for the very first time. It was so special—like sisters would do, I guess. I never had another woman care like that, one who wanted to teach me things.

Later, when I was heading back home, Patsy hugged me and said, "Here ya go—a little gift." She handed me a little brown sandwich bag. Inside was my very own razor. I never had one of those before. I didn't have makeup or girly things like that back then. I knew Doo wouldn't like me shaving, so when I got home I hid that razor.

We'd married so young, I was just barely a woman. Doo said he knowed what he wanted in a wife when he got back home from the war in Germany. He saw in me what he wanted, then he more or less raised me, to tell the truth. 'Course I had those four babies so close together. I was a wife and a mother before I was twenty-two. In Washington I tried to be a good wife to him. He never made it easy, but I tried. Now he was having a hard time with all the changes in our lives. He felt he was losing control over me. And he was.

Things like me wearing makeup and going off without him all the time didn't sit well with him, I guess. It made me feel guilty, if you want to know the truth, even though I hadn't done nothin' wrong! When he got mad, he'd go off and drink. He'd come home drunk and I'd get mad about him being drunk. It was this whole crazy cycle. I wanted to, but I just didn't know how to keep him happy.

Anyway, it was wrong of me to hide the razor from Doo. I guess I thought, well, it was a one-time deal. Dang Patsy, she did not tell me once you shave your legs you have to keep it up. When your hair starts growing back it's stubbly. That's how Doo found out.

Not long after that day at Patsy's house I was half asleep layin' in bed with Doo. I rubbed my leg on his. Doolittle jumped up out of bed and flipped on the light so fast I swear I thought we were being robbed. He yanked all the covers off me. "Loretta!" he shouted. "When did you shave your legs?" I told him yes, I shaved them, and that all women do it.

He said, "Why? You never have shaved them before. Who are you shaving your legs for? I want to know!"

I was wide awake then. It made me so mad when he got jealous 'cause I never was the type to run around. I took my marriage vows too serious. So I said, "What do you mean, who am I shaving my legs for? Patsy showed me how to do it," I said. "Patsy said I needed to shave them."

Doo said, "Well, hells bells, Loretta! If Patsy told you to jump off a bridge would you do it?"

"Heck no," I said. "That's silly! Patsy would not ask me to jump off a bridge!"

Then he said, "You'll be cutting your hair off next. Or better yet, shaving it off."

Doo could really be hateful sometimes, I tell you what. He'd shame me like that, act like I was stupid for doing something he didn't like. He knew just how to push my buttons. He stayed mad about me shaving my legs for weeks. Doo never found that razor Patsy gave me. I still have it. I put it in my museum.

Patsy never said a word again about me shaving my legs one way or the other. She never made a joke of me. The last thing she'd do was try to make me feel ashamed. I did catch her one day looking at my legs, just to make sure. Yep, I'd shaved them. I just smiled real big at her.

Most people don't know that Patsy's mommy, Hilda, made Patsy's stage outfits. By the time I'd met Patsy, she'd ditched the cowboy outfits for brocade dresses, gold heels, and tiaras. But I sure was wearing cowboy outfits back then!

Another photo of me taken by Doolittle. That's our bedspread being used as a backdrop, 1959.

This is the first publicity photo that I got to wear lipstick in. I thought I was really something.

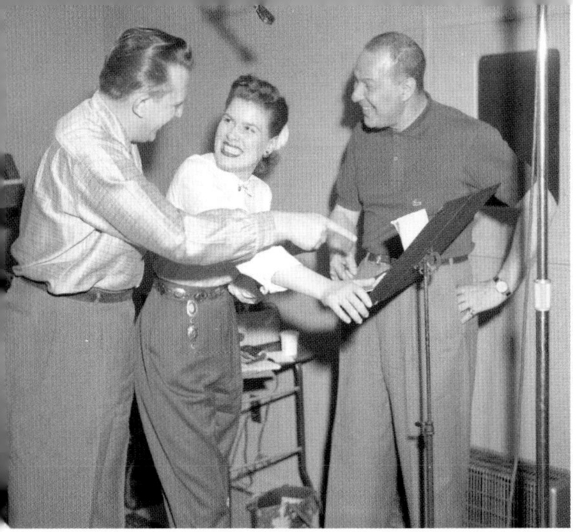

Owen Bradley and Patsy had such a special relationship.

Doyle Wilburn, me, and Teddy Wilburn. These boys did so much for me, and I loved them.

This is the Patsy Cline I got to know best, at home with her babies and her husband, Charlie Dick.

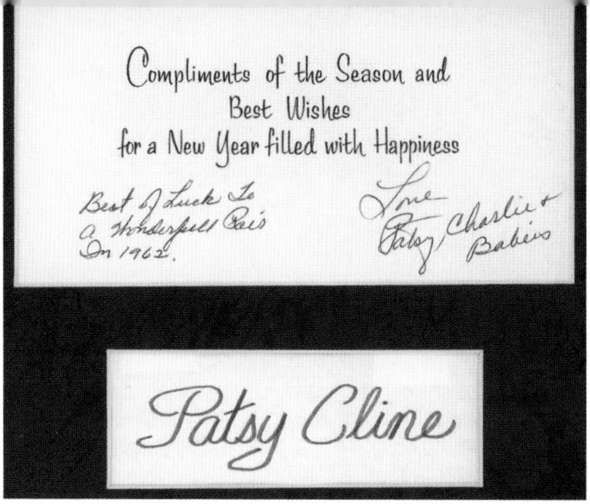
Compliments of the Season and
Best Wishes
for a New Year filled with Happiness
Best of Luck To
a Wonderfull Pair
In 1962.
Love
Patsy, Charlie +
Babies
Patsy Cline

Every year, Patsy took the tim send every one of her friends fans a personalized Christmas card.

In our kitchen in Hurricane Mills, Tennessee, 1966. I know Doolittle is wondering if I'm going to dump this pot of beans over his head! Look at his smile!

Patsy with the Jordanaires. They sang backup on everybody's records, from Patsy Cli to Elvis Presley to me.

Patsy's memorial service showed just a photo of her, and so many flowers. Thousands of flowers.

Not too long after Patsy passed away, I got to record with my hero, Mr. Ernest Tubb. I was pregnant with my twin daughters.

On August 6, 1964, Doo and I had identical twin daughters, Patsy and Peggy.

Premiere of *Coal Miner's Daughter*, 1980. Tommy Lee Jones could not have played Doolittle any better. And Sissy Spacek—y'all know how much I love her!

A 1994 publicity photo for *Honky Tonk Angels*. Me with Dolly Parton and Tammy Wynette—a collaboration with two women who would also have musical breakthroughs soon after Patsy and me.

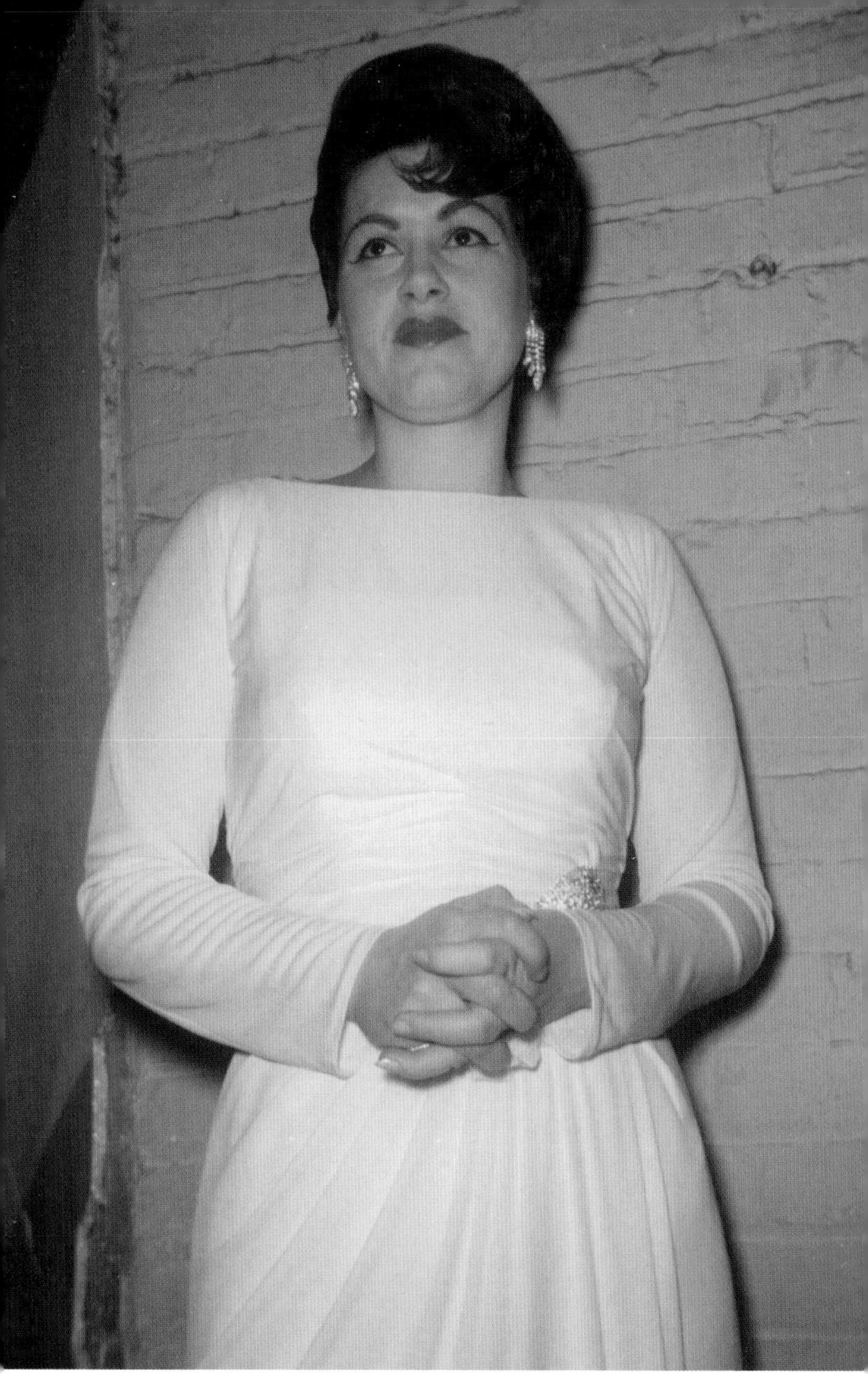

I got to see Patsy try on this dress. We were upstairs in her bedroom. She looked like an angel in it. This is the last photo ever taken of her, in Kansas City.

Like a Sister

I never had a girlfriend before Patsy.

Growin' up in Kentucky, my first cousin, Marie Castle, was my closest friend. We were like sisters. She was Daddy's sister's girl. Her daddy drank quite a bit, but he was mostly a good guy. He'd fought in World War I and had two Purple Hearts, but it must have got to him. When he got to drinkin', he'd take off and leave Marie and her momma for weeks, sometimes even months. So they lived with us more than not.

Me and Marie stayed in trouble all the time. We'd do silly things like making a mess in the kitchen and hidin' when there was work to be done. We'd make a mess out of any chores Mommy gave us to do, like the time we used too much lye washin' the floor. We got to skatin' around on that wet floor and pulled the paint right off it. We got whooped for that.

Marie was about a year younger than me, but that didn't mean a thing to us. You'd think since I was older, I'd a taught Marie a thing or two, but no. She was wiser in the ways of the world. Maybe 'cause of her daddy being gone so much. Like Patsy, Marie had to look out for herself. Maybe that's what made them both so ornery. For example, my mommy smoked, but she wouldn't let any of us smoke. We'd collect snipes for her—that's what Mommy called the butts people left on the ground after they smoked a cigarette—and she'd smoke that leftover tobacco. We kids knew better than to smoke Mommy's tobacco, but Marie got hold of some rabbit tobacco growing wild in a field. Me and her smoked it together. When Mommy caught us, she wore us both out.

When I moved to Washington with Doo, I missed Marie something awful. We were three thousand miles away from each other. We couldn't very well keep in touch. Later, when I come back home, she was the one I wanted to see the most. We'd never been apart before that. When I came back home after all those years, I was nervous. But then I saw Marie and it was like we'd never been apart. Truth is we were still kids. We weren't yet twenty. She got married not long after I come home—married a guy by the name of Delone. Me and Doo went and spent the night with 'em. They lived right out of the holler. The bad thing was, Marie never took care of herself. She smoked and wouldn't give it up. Like Patsy, she died too young.

I recognized that same mouthy attitude in Patsy and it made me like her even more. I'd been looking for a friend like that ever since I left Butcher Holler. She could make me laugh when nobody else could. Patsy and me bonded about husband troubles, too. When I first met Patsy, she saw that Doo was missing his front two teeth. She asked, "What happened to Mooney's mouth?" When I told her the story, she got a kick out of it, so I'll tell it here.

Doo come home one night and I was rockin' little Ernest Ray, my hair up in pin curlers. Doo had promised he'd take me out and I had been looking forward to it all day. Well, he was already drunk when he got home, making all kinds of noise, sayin' he was heading out again. I put the baby down and said, "Mooney Lynn! You promised I could go with you tonight." He said no, I wasn't going anywhere. Just to be ugly, he pulled out one of my pin curlers. I knew then that he was headed out to see some woman. I was mad as a hornet. I fired up and hit Doo square in the mouth—broke his two front teeth. I saw pieces of them fly out and hit the floor. I thought he would kill me, but he was hurt so bad he got to yelling, blood spurtin' everywhere. The babies were all a-cryin'—it was a mess. Doo hollered he needed a dentist. We got that dentist on the phone and when he said he wouldn't see Doo, Doo threatened to kill him! So the dentist finally said to come on over and he pulled the rest of those teeth. Doo went without front teeth for the longest time. I think he liked telling the story. And it kept him from taking up with any other women 'til we could get enough money to fix 'em. That suited me fine.

Patsy laughed hard at that—and she understood it. Our husbands were both characters. Charlie was a ladies' man, too, and he loved a good party. He was loud, always the center of attention. Doo wasn't always the center of attention, but you can bet he thought he was the cutest guy in the room. He'd flirt and carry on. Patsy and me'd just sit back and watch the two of them and laugh.

I have to say, I believe Charlie and Doo were really good for each other. Doo and I hadn't been in Nashville that long and so Doo didn't really have many guy friends. Charlie had a *lot* of friends. Lord, I think Charlie Dick knew everyone in Nashville! He could recall a person's name even if he only met 'em one time. I'm telling you, it was downright impressive. It also came in handy for Patsy because she couldn't remember *anyone's* name! I guess when you'd been performing as long as she had and meeting so many people, you can't store all that information. Charlie and Patsy would be out somewhere and Charlie would say to Patsy, "Patsy, two o'clock, heading your way, that's Dan So-and-So." Those folks would just smile so big because Patsy Cline had called them by name.

Patsy had a wicked sense of humor and she liked to play jokes. One time she called me to come over. When I got to her house I couldn't find her. I looked everywhere. Nothing. Finally I went to the basement. A strange blonde-headed woman was sitting there, just grinning at me. It scared the daylights out of me! Then it dawned on me. It was Patsy! She'd got herself a platinum blonde wig. We both fell down laughing so hard.

When I think back to those days, I think of Patsy laughing and cutting up. There's nothing better than sharing laughs with a good friend.

I learned lots of things from Patsy, just like I would from a sister. She was so much braver than me. She'd have these clothes I'd never seen before—formfitting outfits, panty hose. When I finally did try panty hose myself, I didn't even know they came in sizes. I grabbed the first pair I saw in the store. Those things fell right off me onstage! Patsy had to teach me to look for the right size.

She also taught me about wearing makeup. I'd never worn it before, and the Wilburns had been encouraging me to try it. So one day I was at Patsy's and she let me try some of hers. She showed me how to put on powder, lipstick, mascara, the works. I thought it looked real good. When Doo came to pick me up, he saw right away that something was different. Instead of complimenting me, he shook his head and said, "Loretta, you get in the bathroom and wash that damn shit off your face. You look like a fool!"

Patsy got mad right back. She said, "You leave her alone, Hoss. Loretta's in show business and she's gonna wear makeup."

He let up eventually and I started wearing makeup.

Patsy was real generous about sharing her success and lifting me up when she could. Like in the early days, when I was just starting to get on the radio. Let me tell you this, it was a real big deal to get disc jockeys to like you because they loved country music more than anybody. They really did. Weren't no iTunes back then, just boys sitting in tiny booths for hours, spinnin' records, no air-conditioning or nothing. They just sat there taking phone calls and record requests. They got to know real quick which songs folks liked and which they didn't, and even *why* they didn't like a song. I respected that. Maybe it's because in my heart, I was still a girl listening to Daddy's ole radio, waiting to hear the man say, "Now here's a new song by the Carter Family." And I was still that lonesome housewife, singin' along with Webb Pierce to "There Stands the Glass." So those boys spinnin' their records were real special to me. Little stations, big stations. I didn't care—I loved them all.

Patsy's hits meant she was on the radio a lot, doing interviews with DJs and talking to her fans. When she had a chance, Patsy used her publicity to help me. I remember the time a radio show called her up at her house, asking if she'd come on in to be on their show. They didn't have ways back then for you to call in—you had to go into the station. Patsy looked over at me and said, "You want me to come on? Sure! And you're going to have Loretta on, too, Hoss." That's the kind of friend she was.

Stickin' It to the Haters

I got to perform on the Opry show something like seventeen times. Every time I did it, I was thrilled to death to be there. Sometimes, though, I'd hear talk backstage that made me madder than a wet hen.

"Have you seen Patsy Cline? She looks a mess!"

"Who's she trying to kid with that wig?"

"That face'll never be the same. Her career is finished!"

It made me so mad! I wanted to give those gossips a piece of my mind, but I kept my mouth shut. I had all the faith in the world that Patsy would make a full recovery, come back on, and show them. Then they could shove it up their rears.

I never said one word to Patsy about what I'd heard backstage or who'd said it. What good would it do? It would only have hurt her. Even though she put on the brave front, I knew the truth: Patsy was afraid. Afraid that she wouldn't be able to sing like she had. Afraid she'd never be pretty enough. Afraid that all she'd worked for would be gone—kaput—after she'd come so far.

Since I didn't know Patsy before, I had nothing else to go on. I'd only ever seen her with that scar on her face and the limp and all the pain. But she remembered the old Patsy, the before-the-accident Patsy. It was hard for her to accept that this was her new normal.

Maybe that's one reason our friendship was so special. I wasn't judging her on who she used to be. Some of the others encouraged her to have plastic surgery, but I accepted and loved who she was as she was. I'd support her no matter what.

I didn't have to wait long for those haters to get their just deserts. Decca released Patsy's single of "Crazy" in October 1961 and it went straight up the country music charts. People couldn't get enough of it, and not just country music folks, either. It was a hit on country music radio, pop radio, and adult contemporary. It'd only been a few months since her number one hit with "I Fall to Pieces"—and here she was with another. With those "back-to-back hits," Patsy got the attention of the label executives who'd always said investing in women was a bad bet. Here's what they did: They started calling her their Decca Darling.

On October 21, 1961, Patsy walked out onto the Opry stage—*without* crutches. That was the first time she performed "Crazy" for the Opry audience, and I'm telling you, that crowd went nuts. They gave her three standing ovations! It was clear from the start she had something special with that song. Patsy walked off the stage with tears in her eyes, real emotional. She took my hands in hers and she said, "I guess that's gonna be my song!"

Carnegie Hall

At the Country Music Festival, the nation's country music DJs announced they'd voted Patsy their Favorite Female Artist. Patsy couldn't believe she'd unseated the reigning queen of country music, Kitty Wells. Kitty held that title for ten years in a row. Still having trouble with her leg, Patsy walked up to receive her award using her crutches. I can remember she wore a pretty aqua-blue lace dress Hilda had made. Funny how you don't forget things like that. And she had to keep going up for awards on her crutches. *Billboard* magazine named her the Favorite Female Country & Western Artist. Then *Music Reporter* gave her their Star of the Year Award.

She was so happy! Patsy told reporters, "My new house is going to have wall-to-wall awards! But what am I gonna do next year?"

Patsy's dreams were coming true and I couldn't have been happier.

And I think she was even happier for me. The country music DJs voted me Most Promising Country Female Artist. At the end of the ceremony, Patsy hugged me.

"You'll be getting this award next year, Little Gal," she said.

"Kitty Wells had it for ten years. It's your turn. There's no way I'll be getting it anytime soon, if ever," I said.

Just a few days later, Patsy stepped aboard a chartered jet headed to New York City. The Grand Ole Opry show was playing Carnegie Hall! There's a picture I love of Patsy laughing on the stairway ramp of that plane with Minnie Pearl, Grampa Jones, Bill Monroe, Jim Reeves, and Faron Young. I'll bet those "hillbilly" stars laughed all the way to City Hall, where they were each given a golden key to the city. What a hoot! There was a lot of press there and everybody wanted to talk to Patsy. Usually Patsy loved talking to reporters, but that day she scooted out as quick as she could. Patsy had her momma flown up for the big day. She wanted to spend some time with her momma in the Big Apple before the show.

Patsy said Carnegie Hall was the prettiest venue she'd ever seen—and she'd seen hundreds. She said as she looked out at the four-decked auditorium, decorated in lush reds, "All I could think about was all the famous musicians who'd performed there. What a rush!"

That night Patsy Cline fans came out to the show in full force. There were over forty acts, and she was one of the closers. She was proud of how far she'd come. In my mind, I can just imagine Patsy putting down her crutches to walk onstage to sing in her new stiletto heels. By all accounts, Patsy Cline kept those New Yorkers on their heels, too.

Dirty Old Men

I didn't travel alone. Doo was like my manager for those first few years. He drove me and traveled with me all the time. Folks knew he was my husband, so, mostly, men didn't try anything funny. Now and then some guy who'd been drinking might try and hug me or something. I kept my distance pretty good. I steered clear of trouble. But since men saw that my husband was around, that kept them from getting overly friendly.

It's funny the things you take for granted. I'd been listening to the Opry for so long somehow it seemed like all the men on the Grand Ole Opry were respectable. They all seemed like family, like you could trust 'em. And, in fact, some Opry stars actually have become like family to me now. But at the time, I'd built up a few of them in my mind. I had them on a pedestal. And like Patsy used to say, "You know what birds do to anything on a pedestal, right?"

Bill Monroe was famous where I come from. He was the father of bluegrass and he had more clout than the governor. I mentioned him in that last chapter. He's one of the greatest bluegrass pickers and singers that ever lived. The day I met him I was so dang excited I was grinnin' ear to ear. I played a package show in the Midwest along with a few other artists, and Bill was on the bill. He was so nice. He took his time standing there talking with me. It was an honor, really, 'cause it felt like we were two musicians, talking. He'd heard I was from eastern Kentucky and he liked that. He said he liked my singing. I couldn't believe he'd even heard me sing, much less liked it! I guess I got to talking a mile a minute. I hugged him. I said, "I can't wait until I tell my mommy I met you. She is your biggest fan." I gave him another hug before saying good-bye. As I turned my back to leave, Bill reached down and pinched my butt, *hard*.

I just kinda froze. Nothing like that had ever happened to me before. I didn't say a word. I took off walking as fast as I could to the little dressing area some of us girls all shared. Nobody was in there, so I sat down and cried my eyes out. I thought, *Now why did he do that?* Was it because I hugged him? Oh God, did he think I was flirting with him? It seemed like it had to be my fault. Otherwise how could a respectable man like Bill Monroe do such a thing? I was so young and naive. Now I know better. Bill was a dirty ole man, plain and simple. Being talented didn't make him trustworthy or a gentleman. I don't like it, but I know now. You can't trust somebody just 'cause you wish you could. People will show you their true colors if you let 'em.

Back then a lot of men thought they got a free pass to do whatever they wanted because of who they were or how much money they had. But that's wrong. I am so proud of those who have spoken up about this kind of behavior. It takes guts.

I couldn't tell Doolittle about Bill Monroe. He would have broke all his fingers, and that could ruin us in the music business. So I told Patsy everything. The whole story, front to finish. I cried, asking, "Was it my fault? What should I do?"

"Hell no, it's not your fault!" Patsy said. "When men do those kinds of things, you gotta set them straight, Little Gal. These performers like to see what they can get away with. You stand up to them. Show them you don't go for that kind of thing." Then she smiled with a little wink and said, "Unless you want 'em to pinch ya."

Lord, that Patsy! She could be a rascal.

"But really," she said. "If that happens again, you kick the fire out of them. That'll show 'em." I took every word Patsy said to heart. Nobody could touch me unless I said so.

I was ready the next time it happened. It must have been the winter of 1961. Nashville winters aren't too bad, but this night was a cold one—the kind of cold you feel in your bones. Charlie, Patsy, Doo, and I rode over together to the Opry. Patsy wasn't playing that night, just me. Charlie parked a long way from the back door of the Ryman. I was dressed in just my stage outfit. I didn't have a coat on. I must have left it at home when Charlie and Patsy pulled in to pick us up. Charlie always laid on the horn like a bus just to aggravate us. When we got to the Opry, Doo and Charlie headed straight to Tootsies.

Tootsies Orchid Lounge is legendary now. It's huge—three stories tall and three stores wide. It got its name when Hattie Louise "Tootsie" Bess bought that little ole hole-in-the-wall honky-tonk with a sign out front that said MOM'S. Tootsie hired somebody to paint it, and that painter mixed together a bunch of leftover paint. It come out that purple color. Tootsie was a character. She liked it and dubbed the place "Tootsies Orchid Lounge."

Since the Grand Ole Opry show was at the Ryman, right across the alley, artists would duck out in between shows for a beer or two at Tootsies. Nashville locals weren't too keen on country music. So Tootsies got to be a place where country musicians and writers hung out. The dozen or so country music songwriters would be there on the weekends, when Opry musicians came by, so they could pitch their songs. Bobby Bare, Tom T. Hall, Roger Miller, Harlan Howard, Hank Cochran—all those greats hung out there.

So that night, Doo and Charlie headed over to have a drink, play a little pinball. Me and Patsy would meet up with them later.

I remember it was cold and windy and the back entrance to the Ryman was packed with fans. Security had roped off a path so the artists could get to the backstage area. Patsy and I were weaving our way through the crowd. Not many folks knew me yet, but everyone knew who Patsy

Cline was. They started hollering her name. Flashbulbs were going off—flash, flash! It was crazy and exciting. But I was freezing to death. I wanted to get inside and warm up. We'd made it to the top steps backstage and there was Faron Young, holding the door open for us. Faron was so handsome folks called him "the Hillbilly Heartthrob." He truly did look like a movie star. As Patsy headed through the door, he smacked her on the behind. Well, I hadn't recovered from the whole Bill Monroe ordeal and Patsy's words still rang in my ears. She hadn't asked for that. I hauled off and kicked Faron Young hard as I could in the shin. I said, "Keep your hands to yourself, buddy!" As soon as I did it, I thought, *Bad move, Loretta*. Faron yelled, "Ouch!" While he stood there, rubbing his leg, Patsy doubled over laughing. She said, "That'll teach ya! Don't mess with Loretta!" He might have been mad, but Faron said, "I like you, Loretta Lynn!" Patsy said, "Me too. Me too."

A lot of men chased us girl singers, on and off the road—and I mean chased. Vern Young once said my "little tail" looked good in any dress, then ran me around a desk half a dozen times trying to kiss me. He never did catch me. If he had, I'd have smacked him. I learned to stand my ground. I had my guitar and I'd bust it over somebody's head if I had to. I would have.

Years later, I was on the *Frank Sinatra Show*. I was supposed to do a duet with Dean Martin. Well, Dean never did show up for rehearsals. We were working on the choreography for the number and they told me Dean was supposed to twirl me around and we'd end with me on his lap. "The heck we will!" I said. I couldn't believe it. "My momma taught me never to sit in no man's lap. I never even saw my momma sit in my daddy's lap, and I ain't gonna sit in Dean Martin's lap."

I sang my duet with Dean Martin standing next to him and we never touched.

After we taped the show, I walked into my dressing room and there were so many roses in there I couldn't hardly turn around. The show's producer had sent 'em. He said, "I have to meet the little girl who wouldn't sit in Dean's lap."

Patsy would've loved that.

Homewreckers

As I've said before, I was always faithful to Doo. But that don't mean I was naive. I knew then what I know now: There are women out there who don't care if a man is married or not. 'Course there are men that don't care if a woman is married, either. Either way, they're called homewreckers. They don't care about the families and children that get wrecked. I know all about country music hoes. They'd hang around Tootsies or in Printers Alley in Nashville and of course when I'd tour there were always groupies hanging around after the shows, waiting to see who they might hook up with in the motels or bars. So many homes got broken up from affairs. I just hate it.

The biggest songs I have written over my career have been about these kinds of things. Lord knows I have lived through a lot of what I write and sing about. Cheating is one of 'em.

What I have learned is this: If your husband or wife cheats on you, that's on them. It's their own fault and it has nothin' to do with you. They made a promise—

why anybody would break a promise like that is a mystery to me. Friends, they say the grass looks greener on the other side of the fence, but they soon find it's just as hard to mow.

Me and Doo stayed together through all his misbehaviors because I always fought for our marriage. When women tried to get with my man, I let them know to back off. Mess with my husband and family—oh, no! And don't think for a minute I let Doo off the hook when he stepped out on me, either. I loved Doo and I respected him, but I didn't let him get away with cheating. For years I'd fuss and holler and hit, trying to make him stay true. It didn't make any difference. But once I got to be a singer, I wrote songs as my payback. I wrote "You Ain't Woman Enough," "Fist City," and on and on. He knew I was singing about him. Those songs all became hits, too, so the whole world knew what Doolittle Lynn had been up to. My fans knew I wrote what was happening in my life. My therapy was his payback, so to speak.

You know, Doolittle never did say a word to me about those songs. Never got mad, not one time. He'd say, "I think that's a great song, honey! It's a hit." Maybe he knew I needed that outlet to work through the hurt.

Patsy once told me, "Loretta, you can't just go around threatening to yank a bimbo's hair out of their head for flirting with your husband." My answer was "The heck I cain't." I was scrappy, always have been. I think that's one of the reasons Patsy liked me. I'm sweet until you give me reason not to be. If you cross me and my family,

Lord, you better watch out! I was never a screaming-and-yelling kind—I think that's stupid. I would just haul off and whack ya. My motto was: Hit first and make the first hit count.

Patsy wasn't like me that way. Her husband, Charlie Dick, was a really handsome man. And, as I have said before, he was the life of the party. Funny, smart—he just had a charm about him everyone loved. Women flirted with him right and left, all the time. I'd say, "Patsy, that ole girl is flirting with Charlie!" She' d say, "Aw, he's okay." What the heck? If that was Doo I would have been in that gal's face in a heartbeat. I know jealousy is a bad thing to have. Still, I'm a jealous wife. Always have been. Patsy never got that upset about Charlie flirting, at least not that I saw. She'd just go on with whatever she was doing. She paid no mind to all the female attention Charlie was getting. I can't say the same for myself.

Neither me nor Patsy liked to eat before we sang, so after a show we'd both be starving to death. A lot of times after the *Midnite Jamboree* we'd head over to this little diner on Fourth and Broad called Linebaugh's. We'd grab a late-night burger or hot dog or one of their sugar doughnuts—anything to fill us up. It was always pretty packed at Linebaugh's, so you'd order your food and wait. One night Patsy must have been scheduled to sing or somethin', 'cause me and Charlie went over there, just the two of us. We took a seat to wait while they were cooking our order. All of a sudden this woman comes through the door, walks straight up to Charlie Dick, and sits down in his lap. I mean, plops right down into his lap! She looked like a made-up, high-class streetwalker. I'm sure my mouth fell open so wide I could have swallowed a fly. This ole gal didn't even look my way. No hello, not a smile, nothing. It was like I wasn't even there. Why, she was too busy rubbing up against Charlie. Like I said, he was a flirt, so this was just fine with him.

Now, Charlie wasn't my husband and I reckon it wasn't my right to say or do anything, but it burned me up how this strange woman just waltzed in and started hangin' all over my friend's husband. Besides, from what I could tell, she seemed to know Charlie and be familiar with the country music folks. So she must have known Charlie was Patsy's husband. She cooed, "Oh, Charlie, you're so funny, ah ha ha."

No way, I thought. *Not on my watch.* I stood up and waved my hand in front of this gal's face to get her attention. I said, "Hi, how are ya? I am a friend of Charlie's and Patsy's—that's his wife." I did not tell her my name. She kinda looked me up and down, if you can call it that. Then she took my outreached hand to shake it. She said in a real smart-aleck way, "Look at your little white cowboy boots. Aren't those cute?" She was trying to make fun of me. I thought, *Oh no you don't!* So with my best hillbilly, don't-know-nothing-about-nothing accent, I said, "I'm so sorry, but I'm about to wet myself. Do you mind helping me find the bathroom in this place? I would be so grateful to ya." Now, I'd been to Linebaugh's plenty of times before and once I'd mistakenly opened a broom-closet door on the way to the ladies' room. So I had an ace up my sleeve.

It would have been really rude for her to tell me no, but, trust me, if that didn't work I would have came up with something else. I didn't need to worry, though, because this hussy bought it—hook, line, and sinker. She got up and went with me. We darted in and out of people as she directed me on where to go. Soon as I reached the broom closet, I said, "Oh, I see it, thank you so much," and I walked straight inside. It was pitch black in there. I heard her holler "That's not it!" She opened the door to tell me I was in the wrong room. She said, "Where's the light?" Just as she walked far enough in, I pushed her back inside that closet and slid right around her. I shut the door fast and locked it. She knocked on the door and started hollering, but I just walked away. I got back in time to see Charlie paying for our food at the counter. I gave him a big smile and we left together, headed back to Patsy.

Charlie never did ask where that gal went, so I never said nothing about it. Who knows how long she was in there—a minute? An hour? Couldn't have been too long. Maybe somebody heard her hollering and let her out. Linebaugh's was a small place. I didn't tell Patsy, either. I didn't want to get her and Charlie into a fuss.

A few days later, Patsy called me up on the phone. She said she'd heard that a big-shot record VP's wife was found locked in the broom closet at Linebaugh's the other night. "Really?" I said, thinking, *Oh shoot! I locked a big-shot VP's wife in the broom closet!* Patsy said, "Charlie told me you and him saw her the other night when you were picking up our food." I held my tongue. Patsy laughed then. She said, "You don't know anything about it, now do ya, Loretta?" There was no way to get out of confessing, so I started apologizing a mile a minute. "Oh, Patsy, I am so sorry. I didn't know who she was. She walked in and sat right down in Charlie's lap and was carrying on and I just..." I was near tears.

Patsy stopped me. She said, "Hey now, it's okay! I'm getting a kick out of this. You did good, Loretta."

I was glad Patsy wasn't mad at me, but I was worried. What if that old gal recognized me? But ya know what? To this day, thank goodness, I never heard from her again. Maybe she pulled the same stunt and somebody else's wife locked that ole ho in a closet in Mexico or somewhere else far away from Nashville.

Bad Detectives

I was trying to do it all, to be a superwoman. Writing my own songs, doing shows, and still holding things at home together—cooking, cleaning, keeping four kids washed and fed and clothed. I was tired about all the time. Burning out fast. One day I came home from another road tour with the Wilburns and Doo took off like a rocket. It was like his shift was over and the whistle blew. It made me so mad! I thought, *Doolittle's free as a bird, going out to have a good ole time, leaving me at home having to do everything else.* Again. Just like in Washington state.

The difference this time was I was busting my tail to make it in the music business. It was hard work. Add four kids on top of all that and, trust me, it wasn't easy.

So Doo's shenanigans did not sit well with me. The next morning, I asked what he'd been doing out so late. He said, "Me and Doyle was just having a few beers, honey. Time got away from us." When I asked him where they'd been, he got mad at me for even asking. He said, "Woman, you ain't my keeper!" I said, "Like hell I'm not!"

Later that afternoon after he left, I took a cab over to Patsy's to help her pack for her trip. I told her how irritated I was with Doo. My mind started running wild with all kinds of crazy thoughts. I said, "Patsy, what if he has a girlfriend again? Here I am working my tail off and he's running around on me!" The more I talked the more I got worked up. Patsy tried to calm me down, but I was too worked up. Finally she said, "Loretta, where's Mooney right now?" I said, "Heck if I know! Probably out with a big old blonde bimbo." The tears started rolling. Lord, I was a mess, carryin' on.

Patsy stood up and hollered for Charlie. She yelled, "Charlie, start the car!" Patsy said, "Come on, Loretta. Let's do us a little detective work. If Mooney's out there, we'll find him." Charlie poked his head in and said, "What's up?"

Patsy said, "Charlie, Loretta is feeling down so we are going to cheer her up. Let's take her for a ride downtown, show her the city lights." She turned to me and said, "Loretta, you ever seen Printers Alley at night? It's a hoot." Then she winked at me—in other words, *Hush*. I thought, *Lord have mercy*.

Me, Patsy, and Charlie all loaded up in their car and headed for downtown, the three of us in the front seat. Charlie had the radio on and music was playing. I can remember Buck Owens's "Act Naturally" was out around that time, and that was on the radio. We weren't really talking, just letting the music fill up the silence. I'd dried my tears, but I was still upset. I thought, *What if we do find Doolittle? What then?* I hadn't really planned on tracking him down. In fact, I hadn't planned this at all. Did I really want to know if he was with another woman? What would I do? What would Doo do when he saw me? My big mouth had really gotten me into a fix this time.

Once we got downtown, Patsy acted like a tour guide, telling me little things about this place and that place. All along I was on the lookout for Doo's car. Even though we both performed at the Ryman on the Opry, downtown Nashville wasn't someplace we went for the views. There were mostly bars down there at the time. It was a little dicey, to tell the truth. We couldn't get out and walk down Printers Alley. Patsy was still having a hard time walking without crutches. But we drove past so I was looking out the window for any sign of Doo.

We rode around like that for maybe an hour with no luck seeing Doo or his car. I wasn't sure whether that was a good or bad thing. Charlie drove me on back to my house so I wouldn't have to get a cab back from their place. Well, as we drove up, there in our driveway on Barber Drive sat Doo's car. Charlie parked in the drive and all three of us walked in together. The kids were home and Doo had cooked dinner, fed everybody, and even cleaned up the kitchen. Talk about feeling bad! When I walked in I gave him the biggest hug! Doo looked at me so funny. Then danged if Charlie Dick didn't tell Doo how Patsy'd made him drive all over downtown Nashville looking for him. I almost died. I could've kicked Charlie right in the shin for telling on us! He knew the whole time what me and Patsy was up to. We hadn't got away with one thing. I was ready for Doo to be mad at me, but he wasn't. In fact, I think he liked that I was jealous of him. As Patsy and Charlie left, Doolittle said to me, "You sure are cute when you get caught checking up on me." I said I didn't know what in the world Charlie was talking about. Patsy and I just wanted to go for a little ride to see all the lights. Doolittle just smiled and said, "Sure you did, Loretta. Sure you did."

Man of the House

Men ran the show in country music in the sixties, just like everywhere else. They booked the shows, signed songwriters to music publishing deals, gave singers recording contracts, produced the music, and decided what to play on the radio. I'd been bossed by Doo since I was a girl. Now the Wilburns were bossing me. Seemed like men were forever telling me what I could and couldn't do.

And you have to remember, married women back then were called "housewives." I guess "keeping house" was considered a woman's job, and her boss was her husband. It sounds crazy, I know. Trying to be a wife while having a career wasn't normal yet. What me and Patsy were doing was just making it up as we went along. There wasn't any map.

I couldn't have been working if it weren't for Doo being there for our kids. He'd gotten me into the music business to start with, and his support made it so I could work. In those days it was rare for a man to take care of kids. That was considered a woman's work, to be at home to put them to bed and wake them up in the mornings, make sure they were fed. But my husband did it.

Plus Doo knew how to take care of me better than anybody. When I came in from a long road trip, bone-tired and hungry, he'd fix me a big bowl of beans with a chopped-up yellow onion on top. We'd been together so long that what we had wasn't just romantic. We were family.

I'm not saying it was easy. Doo drank too much. And he acted the fool plenty. We had lots of knock-down, drag-out fights over the years. But he deserves credit for my success. I hate double standards, and that there's even a double standard. When a woman stands behind her husband and he gets successful, she gets respect and attention. Why don't men get the same? Somehow when a wife has success, it's like the man gets the short end of the stick.

It looked like I had a chance to be a success in this business, and I sure wasn't gonna let that tear me and Doo apart. That's one reason I liked it when Decca released my next single, "Success," in April 1962. Johnny Mullins was the writer. It made sense to me to sing about how success can tear a couple apart when one of them gets ahead in this world. The song went to number six on the charts and I'd say that's a success, wouldn't you?

Patsy and Charlie hadn't been married near as long as me and Doo. Next to us, they were newlyweds. But I can tell you, they loved each other like crazy. Sure, they fussed and fought, but just try and stand between them. You'd get knocked down! The way I see it, only two people know the truth about a marriage, and that's them that's in it.

Yes, it's true Charlie was a big joker and the life of every party, but there was a real sad part of Charlie. He loved

Patsy so much but he could be mean sometimes—and I mean *mean*. No one would know when or what would set Charlie off, but when he got mad, the party was over. As I've said, Patsy never told me that Charlie hit her, but Doo thought he did. When he told me that, I couldn't believe it. I didn't want to believe it.

Patsy was a proud person, and she kept that all to her own self. Likely as anything, when she called to complain about Charlie, the first words out of her mouth to me might be "Charlie is a big SOB!" and nine times out of ten she'd end up sayin', "I gotta go, Charlie's on the way home. I got to get supper on." The next day, they couldn't keep their hands off each other. That was just the way it was with them.

There was one thing Doo and Charlie had in common that I wish they didn't. Other men gave them a hard time about living off Patsy's and my money. Like I even had any money back then! Charlie, mostly he'd let any smart comments roll off his back. He'd laugh. Not Doolittle. Make fun of him and he'd punch your lights out. You couldn't get away with calling him "Mr. Loretta Lynn." He'd fight you for it and earned a reputation as a hothead.

I understood why he got so mad. Doo worked hard his whole life. It hurt his pride when folks thought he was bumming off me. What they didn't know is I'd be nothing in my career without him. I wouldn't have been singing, much less hanging out with Patsy Cline and Charlie Dick. When somebody kidded him about being Mr. Loretta Lynn, it made me mad, but it made me love him even more.

Working Moms

I was on the road a lot in 1962. My managers believed I had raw talent, lots of energy, and a strong work ethic. What I needed was to learn how to perform for audiences—not just sing, but perform. I understood what they meant because I'd watched Patsy connect with audiences. They hung on her every note. Watching her inspired me.

As part of my training, the Wilburns sent me on a tour of state fairs. I got a crash course in making do on that tour! I'd show up someplace and, heck, there might not even be a stage. Or they'd have me perform next to the livestock exhibition. These may not have been the most glamorous of venues, but it gave me a real education. One night the Wilburns called me onstage when I was getting ready. My hair was still in curlers. They wanted to see how well I'd do under pressure. We kinda bantered onstage. The audience liked it, I think, and it encouraged me.

It was a crazy schedule. I played forty-two shows in twenty-five days—a jam-packed tour. The good news was,

I made fifty dollars a show. Me and Doo thought we was rich!

The singing and playing my guitar came easy. The rest of it took a while to get the hang of. Doo used to tease to get me to smile walking out onstage. Smiling didn't always come easy, especially if I had a headache or the weather was bad or I was missing my kids.

I called Patsy for some advice. She said, "Start with a fast song that gets their blood pumping." Even after she discovered her gift for ballads, Patsy'd start her shows with an up-tempo, fun song like "Come On In." That made folks feel excited to be there, no matter what kind of day they'd had so far. She said, "After you have their attention, make them fall in love with you with the slow ones." Talk to them and the band, she said. And leave them wanting more.

After weeks doing fairs, the Wilburns arranged for me to join a package tour booked by the famous promoter Hap Peebles. Then my second single, "Success," came out and reached number six on the charts. My first to hit the top ten! From then on, we played in venues that were a little nicer, like auditoriums and clubs.

When I wasn't on the road, I was writing for Sure-Fire. That's where I met Betty Sue Perry. Sure-Fire had hired her to write songs like they'd hired me. I liked Betty Sue's lyrics. They felt true to me. I liked them so much I recorded some of her songs. Four of them ended up being top twenty, and "Wine, Women and Song" even got up to number three in 1964. Sure-Fire signed Betty Sue to a lifetime contract, like they did me. Sad to say, Betty Sue got sick and passed away in 1974. I'm glad I got to work with her at a time when most all the writers in country music were men. Men are no good at writing from a woman's perspective and telling their stories.

While I was learning the basics of performing and learning to write lyrics I could believe in, Patsy was taking performing to a whole new level. She'd long ago learned how to outperform any artist out there. Talk about stage presence! When Patsy walked onstage, you couldn't take your eyes off her. And when she sang, *shoot*. You hardly knew what hit you. Her voice was so strong, so emotional.

In 1962 she was having her best year yet professionally. Her career was white hot. She was the top female singer in country music. And it wasn't just country. Everybody loved her. Nobody would've believed a woman singer could accomplish all the things Patsy had done. She had a string of hits, "Crazy," then "Strange" and "She's Got You." She was on a roll! After years of fighting to get respect and attention from the label heads, she was the "Decca Darling." I was so proud of her.

One day Patsy called me up with some news. Johnny Cash had invited her to tour with the *Johnny Cash Show*. Johnny had left Nashville and was living out in California by then. Cash was Patsy's kind of country music star—a rebel who made his own rules.

Her first performance with Johnny Cash was in January 1962. When Johnny announced her, he didn't call her sweet or pretty or cute. He gave her the respect she deserved. He said, "Ladies and Gentlemen—the one, the only—Patsy Cline." That was a real compliment. It was his way of saying *Patsy Cline isn't just another girl singer. She's special.* Patsy knew it, too. From then on, that's how Cash announced her.

So while I was singing in county fairs, Patsy was performing with superstars like Johnny Cash, June Carter, George Jones, Carl Perkins, and a teenager named Barbara Mandrell. It was just the two-week tour at first. After that they booked Patsy whenever they could. Sometimes it'd be a one-nighter. Other times she'd get on a bus with the "Johnny Cash family" and they'd go on a ten-city tour.

In June she flew out to the West Coast to sing with Johnny Cash at the Hollywood Bowl. They called it the *Shower of Stars*. Over forty-two artists performed that night, but Patsy got top billing, second only to the Man in Black himself. It was real unusual for a woman to get billing next to a man that way. Again, Patsy was blazing a trail for the rest of us.

"I've been telling Randy I want to slow down some," she told me on the phone. "But with four hits in a row, and now the Hollywood Bowl behind me, he's asking top dollar for my appearances. And getting it! A thousand dollars!"

"Patsy, a thousand dollars? For one show?"

"Can you believe it? I'd be a fool not to take that. You gotta make hay while the sun's shining."

"Can't you cut a few more records? Stayin' off the road ain't the same as sitting still."

"Performing and meeting fans are what sell records,

Little Gal. If I don't go out, the records I make won't sell. No, I just have to suck it up. But I sure do miss my babies!"

It was a lot to juggle, touring, keeping house, and raising a family. There was always so much to do the minute we got home. Neither of us had a housekeeper or a nanny. So when we got together, we'd work side by side, cleaning, cooking, doing laundry.

In a way I think Patsy had it worse than me. Julie wasn't old enough for school, and Randy was a baby. At least my kids were big enough to fend for themselves if they had to. Sometimes Patsy'd call home twice a day just to hear their little voices. It broke her heart to leave them with a babysitter, especially if one was sick.

When one of my kids got sick while I was away, I felt so guilty. I'd boss everybody over the phone and then hang up and worry. And pace. And worry some more. Sometimes it felt like I was going nuts. When I was working, I wished I was home. When I was at home, I wished I was makin' music. I wanted to be in two places at once.

I came home from a tour in Texas once. I'd been gone for two weeks and all I could think about was getting home. My vegetables needed puttin' up, I had cannin' to do, and the kids needed this and that. But first I planned to make my family a nice big country dinner. I even knew what I wanted to make.

Doo had been working on the house while I was gone, fixing some things. He was handy. He could do anything. So when I got home, Doo had to show me what he'd done. He was so proud. Everything looked nice and I told him so. Then I said, "That's enough showin' off, Doo. I'm ready to get in the kitchen and cook you a big meal!" Cooking would take my mind off things and help me relax. Feeding people makes me happy.

I walked in that kitchen and it felt good at first. But then I started spinnin' in circles. Every cupboard door I opened was the wrong one. I got more and more confused. I couldn't find any of my own pots and pans! All I wanted to do was cook and I couldn't put my hands on a blame thing I needed. Somehow that cut me down to the core. I dropped to the floor and cried.

I'd been away so long, I didn't even know my own dang kitchen.

Dream Home

In May 1962, the summer after the wreck, Charlie was driving Patsy around Nashville. For months they'd been searching for the perfect house. All of a sudden Patsy hollered for Charlie to stop and pointed to a house she'd seen. Charlie saw that the house was still under construction, but they got out and looked around anyway.

It was a split-level brick house on a nice-sized piece of property. For Patsy it was love at first sight. She just had to have it. Charlie argued it was awfully big and it might be too expensive. He told her not to get her hopes up. But Patsy was determined. "We can afford it, Charlie. And if we can't, I'll get Randy to add some more dates."

Patsy got what she wanted.

The house was on Nella Drive in the suburbs just north of Nashville. Patsy was like a kid at Christmas with that house. *Excited* ain't the word! She had a big time, spending all her free moments decorating it just how she liked.

In the living room, there was a fireplace and custom-made three-piece sofa with draperies to match. The master bedroom was beautiful with a huge rug made to look like a gold record. That makes me think about what her house might look like today. With all the records she's sold by now, she'd have gold, platinum, and diamond rugs in her house!

I remember how excited she was about her bathroom. It was her favorite part of the house, I think. She had it done special, modeled after something she'd seen in a movie. "Isn't it glamorous?" she said. And of course it was. There was gold glitter in the white bathroom walls and floor. It sparkled and shined.

My favorite was the music room on the bottom level. There were wood floors and a bar with the words "Patsy and Charlie's" studded into the red leather. Real comfortable. It was perfect for entertaining, which Patsy loved to do.

After Patsy showed me all around that first time, she pulled me by the arm out into the front yard. "Ain't it pretty, Little Gal?" she said. I said it was. We stood there looking at the place, admiring it.

Then she said, "You know I won't be really happy until I get my mama one just like it."

Patsy was so big-hearted.

She called that house on Nella Drive her castle. She told everybody she'd earned it with blood, sweat, and tears. She said, "When I die, y'all can just lay me out right here in this living room."

Nice Things

Patsy was real generous. I hardly ever spent time with her without her sharing a meal or a dress or something. She liked to open up her closet to show off some new pair of shoes, then while she was at it she'd pull out some things she hadn't worn in a while. She'd have them in a bag for me before I left her house. It was just how she was.

One time Patsy came over to visit me at our little rental house over on Barber Drive. I didn't have no curtains hanging on the windows. I didn't mind much—I was used to making do. Patsy went home that day and made me some curtains on her sewing machine! She hated to see somebody go without if she could help it.

Brenda Lee said when she was starting out, she wasn't but twelve or thirteen and in a package show with Patsy out in Texas. This was probably back when Patsy was with 4 Star Records, before I knew either of 'em. Well, the concert promoter run off with all the money. That left Brenda and her mommy pretty well stranded. Patsy didn't miss a beat. She took little Brenda and her momma under her wing, put them in her car, fed 'em, and gave 'em some money. Patsy took care of 'em til they could work a few more dates and get the money to go back home. Patsy'd do anything for anybody.

I think it had to do with her growing up without much. Having to scrap for what she got all those years, Patsy knew what it was to be hungry. It's where a lot of her gumption come from. She didn't want to go back to being hungry.

'Course I know a thing or two about being poor. *Poor* ain't even the word for the way I grew up. Mommy and Daddy didn't have money at all in Butcher Holler. We never lacked for love, but we didn't have nothing much else. Many times we all went to bed hungry. There were some nights Mommy woke us up in the middle of the night 'cause she'd fried up a chicken. She fed us, then sent us back to bed. Later I learned that our cousin Lee Dollarhide stole those chickens when he heard we didn't have enough to eat. When you're hungry, you'll do about anything.

When I go back to the hills to visit, I wonder how in the devil I ever got out. I was lucky. I was poor after that, too, when we moved to Washington state. Remember, I was a housewife and mother for fifteen years before I was an entertainer. I was washing clothes on a washboard and cookin' on an old coal stove. I split logs for the fire in the snow. I planted my own vegetable garden and always put up cans for winter. I raised chickens and killed 'em. All while raising babies and working seven days a week. It was a hard life. But them hard times made me a better person. Made me strong.

Patsy didn't grow up in the woods like me. Still, she didn't have much. I think it might've been harder for Patsy bein' in town. She knew what she didn't have. I never did.

It's no wonder when Patsy started to be successful, she wanted nicer clothes and a nice house. Fancy things tickled her. But what made her happiest was sharing what she had with others.

Happy Thirtieth Birthday

Patsy's third album, *Sentimentally Yours*, released in August 1962. To me, it was her best album yet. It featured the songs "Strange" and "She's Got You." It hadn't been but a year since she'd been wondering if she even had a career anymore. Now she was riding high. To celebrate, and since her birthday was in September, she decided to throw a big house party—the biggest birthday house party you've ever seen. She invited pretty much everybody in country music—and then some.

Country music folks were a pretty tight bunch. Everybody was always traveling, but when we got together, it was like a big reunion. Patsy had her party on a Sunday night so those of us who performed on Friday and Saturday nights could be there.

I went over to help get the house and food ready. She was there in the kitchen dancing to Chuck Berry's record. Patsy knew more about music than anybody I ever met. She took a little bit from all kinds of music—hillbilly music, the blues, R&B, rock and roll, big band. Patsy's sound had something from all those styles. That's what I think, anyway.

By nightfall, all the regulars were there—everybody who wasn't on the road, anyway. Dottie West and her husband, Bill; me and Doo; plus Patsy's manager, Randy, and his wife, Jenny; Hank Cochran and Jeannie Seely; Del Wood; Wilma Burgess; and Teddy and Doyle Wilburn. There were fifty, maybe even seventy-five, other people that came and went.

Somebody brought a guitar and we took turns singing. Doo even tried, but, God bless him, he couldn't carry a tune in a bucket.

Things got a little tense when Charlie brought out some guns he'd "borrowed" from that rascal Faron Young. The two of them got into a tussle about it, but nobody got hurt. Faron liked to show off, that's all, and so did Charlie, so it's no wonder.

That party might have gone on for days, but Charlie had too much to drink. That crazy fool went and mooned everybody! Patsy gave him hell for it. I thought it was kinda funny and told her it made for a memorable night. She said Charlie's ass wasn't what she wanted to be remembered for.

The Cadillac Bitches

I wasn't stupid. I knew people around town called me names like "hillbilly." They made jokes behind my back. I heard them—they wanted me to hear them. They said I couldn't read or speak English. They made fun of my clothes. It's true they were handmade or secondhand outfits, but I was happy to have them. I guess I win on that one, though, 'cause today the new girl singers come down to my ranch and go through my museum to take pictures of those old outfits to copy them for themselves. So THERE!

Now that I had another hit song with "Success," the Wilburns told me the Opry was considering making me a member. I'd been on as a guest a lot, but being invited to be a member was a real big deal. It'd be good for my career. I'd be billed as a "Member of the Grand Ole Opry" and that's about the best publicity you can get. Most performers waited years to be asked, and I'd hardly been in Nashville a year.

Well, that idea started a big old shit storm. Girls started

calling the house, saying I ought to go back out West. Somebody started a rumor saying I slept with somebody to be asked to be an Opry member. What? That was about the furthest thing from the truth. People will just plain make up nonsense when they're jealous. I've figured this out now, but back then I was hurt by it.

Then somebody started a rumor that the Wilburn brothers had paid my way into the Opry. Now, folks, that was pure foolishness. You can't buy your way into the Grand Ole Opry. All of these rumors about wore me out. Where I came from, people celebrated neighbors' successes, they weren't mean about it. This was all new to me. I came home feeling beaten down and discouraged. Do you think I got any sympathy at home? No way! Doolittle got mad at me for letting two-faced people bother me the way they did, but I couldn't help it. Everyone wants to feel accepted. That's how God made us. Doo said, "If you don't quit cryin' I'm gonna take you back to Washington and forget it!" And he would've, too.

So I called Patsy up. She was always on my side. She said, "Heck, Loretta! I say it's better to be talked about than forgotten. Be glad you got those bitches running scared." That made sense to me. It made me feel better to talk to Patsy, anyway. We wound up laughing.

Sometimes folks would whisper, "Loretta Lynn's latched on to Patsy Cline," like I was using Patsy! That made me so dadgum mad I saw red. If they knew Patsy at all they'd know she could not stand fakes. She was a good judge of people. She knew who was real and who wasn't. If they weren't real, they weren't getting a minute of Patsy's time.

Patsy told me some Opry regulars were considering going to Ott Devine. They were going to say that if he kept having me on as a guest, he shouldn't expect them to be available. A boycott, because of me! Well, these ladies invited Patsy to a get-together for what Patsy said would be a "Loretta bitch meeting." I was so hurt. To think Patsy would go hurt my feelings so bad! I was about to let loose when Patsy said, "Don't you worry, Little Gal. You and me are both going to that meeting." She said, "That will shut their asses up."

I didn't want to go. I couldn't see myself walking into the lion's den. But Patsy wouldn't take no for an answer. "Loretta, I've got your back," she said. "You're comin'!" And that was that.

That day we drove up that tree-lined street in Madison. We had the window cracked for a breeze, and I was all nerves, fidgeting around in my seat. When Patsy parked the car, I looked over to her and said, "I ain't never seen so many Cadillacs in all my life." She busted out laughing. I was so nervous, shaking all over, walking into that house. Patsy strolled in like she owned the place, with me in tow. You should've seen the look on some of those gals' faces. *Shock* is the only word I know to describe it. Everyone in that room got quiet. I wondered if somebody might come over and kick me right out that front door.

Patsy looked around and made eye contact with everybody, just a touch of a grin on her face. Then she smiled real nice and said, "Hey, everybody! Y'all know my friend, Loretta?" All of a sudden those faces unfroze. They greeted me like someone they knew forever after that, offering me lemonade and a seat.

The Cadillacs liked me from then on. Patsy's approval was all it took, I guess. I really had a good time, too. I liked all those strong women. To this day when we see each other, we talk and laugh and find out what's new in each other's lives. All because of Patsy.

I can't tell you what it meant to me. And still means. Besides Doo and my family, nobody ever had my back for no other reason than just they loved me. Whatever happened from then on, I'd have done anything for her.

Patsy drove us home that afternoon with the windows down and the radio turned to a country music station, just as loud as you please. We were so young then. There's nothing I wouldn't give to go back to that day.

Member of the Grand Ole Opry

I'd had my sights on being a member of the Opry since I came to Nashville. Now the Wilburns said my dream was about to come true.

Remember how I told about Daddy getting that Philco transistor radio when I was just a girl? Well, back then the Opry had been around awhile. It started in 1925 on a tiny five-thousand-watt station. The National Life and Accident Insurance Company sponsored it. They sold insurance and the call letters were supposed to mean "We Shield Millions"—WSM, get it? They wanted to reach all the states where their agents sold insurance to regular folks—the farm people, the country people.

It was real special from the start. It was my people's music, not city music. The kind of thing you might hear in Butcher Holler where I grew up, or out in other small places. It wasn't polished or what you might call popular. In the 1920s, anybody could be on. It was open call. That ole picker Sam McGee of the McGee Brothers once said folks from the Opry was looking for pickers that was outstanding in the field. "And that's where they found us," he said. "Out standing in the field." That's funny, ain't it? That's the kind of humor Opry folks had. It's true, though. Judge Hay wanted anybody good who could play an instrument or sing old-time country. Anybody that wanted on had to audition for the Judge. It wasn't formal. Come Saturday night Judge Hay might have said who'd be on, or he might wait 'til airtime. He kept folks on their toes. After a while, some of the players got to be regulars, like DeFord Bailey, Uncle Dave Macon, and Dr. Humphrey Bate and His Possum Hunters.

When poor folks learned they could make money making music, they started to line up to audition. It got more competitive. Some of the poor folks who got their start there are now in the Country Music Hall of Fame—folks like Pee Wee King, who played the accordion and was famous for "Tennessee Waltz," and DeFord Bailey, the most amazing harmonica player who ever lived.

When the Opry started taking their shows on the road, they could sell tickets even in the Depression years. The Opry star Roy Acuff was big as Frank Sinatra during the war years. Looking back, it seems like he helped make country music more popular in a lot of ways. He even ran for governor of Tennessee!

The Opry went coast-to-coast in 1943, right around when we Webbs got our radio. Minnie Pearl was the first real comedian on the show. Some of the other stars were Cowboy Copas, Little Jimmy Dickens, Hank Williams, and my favorite, Ernest Tubb. I kept a-listenin' on Saturday nights when me and Doo moved out to Washington state. If I could get to a radio, I'd listen to the Opry show.

Any serious country music entertainer wanted to be an Opry member by the time I got in the business. It was an exclusive club in a way. If they asked you to be a member, you had to commit to being available to perform Saturday nights on the show. In exchange, you could say you were a "Member of the Opry" to advertise and that alone got you good tour dates. There's nothing like an audience of millions to get your name out there! That really helped for booking shows.

The Grand Ole Opry asked me to be a member on September 25, 1962. I was thirty years old. I can't tell you how proud that made me. It was one of the best moments of my life.

The Grand Ole Opry was run by men. Hell, back then most everyplace was! I loved those men, but they made the rules and we had to live by 'em. That's another reason I'm so proud of Patsy. She made her own rules. In the fall of 1959, before I ever saw her, she'd already been on the Opry show a number of times. One night she walked straight up to Ott Devine, who was the stage manager. She told him she wanted to be a full-fledged member of the Grand Ole Opry. Ott said okay. Patsy said, "So, I'm a member now? Just like that?" Ott said, "Yep, just like that." I reckon he knew Patsy was already a star.

Even though it was important to Patsy to be on the

Opry, she wasn't beholden to tradition. Folks like to have a fit when she wore slacks onstage, which back then was downright rebellious. Slacks were for men, especially in Nashville, where people could be real conservative about stuff like that. Patsy always did like to mix things up.

Driving Lessons

When I wanted to visit with Patsy, Doo would drive me. But if he wasn't home I'd take a taxi or she'd send somebody to pick me up. So I wasn't too surprised when one morning Patsy called and said, "I'm sending a car over for you, Little Gal."

"Okay, for what?" I asked.

"I ain't tellin' you 'til you get here. It's a surprise," she said. "You're gonna love it, Loretta. Get your tail dressed and come on over to my house. Taxi will be there in an hour. It's gonna be real fun, you'll see."

Now, I'm thinking, *Okay, we're gonna listen to songs or bake a cobbler maybe*. Or Patsy mighta got some new stage dresses she wants to show me. She was always getting new stage outfits by then. Before the car accident, Patsy had been experimenting with new looks, more sophisticated styles. Now that she was earning more money, she'd gotten even more elegant. She could be real adventurous with her clothes. It was fun to watch. But no, that wasn't it. And "surprise" was right.

When I got to her house, she said, "Loretta, it's time you learned to drive a car."

"No way," I said. "I ain't driving no car. I am scared to death. No one wants me behind a wheel of one of those things. Lord knows I have a hard time just riding with someone else driving."

Growing up in Butcher Holler, we didn't have cars around. The first one I seen was Doo's Jeep when I was thirteen. Doo drove it right up to our house on the hill and told me, "Get in." Ridin' in that Jeep with him was wild. He was a crazy driver then. He loved to go fast. He'd always done the driving in our family.

I wasn't so sure Doo would like me driving and told Patsy so.

Patsy said, "To hell with what Doo wants! What do you want? This is for you, Loretta! You need to learn how to drive. What if you need to go somewhere and Doo's not around?" 'Course that happened a lot and she knew it. She had my number. "If you knew how to drive you could go places without him."

I wasn't convinced. Where would I want to go without Doo? There were many times I wanted to leave him. What if I got it in my head to leave him for real and I could drive? What then? My mind was reelin'. I wasn't sure. That's when Patsy got clever. "What if one of your babies gets sick and Doo ain't there to take you to the hospital?"

She had me there.

"Oh, hell's fire, Loretta! What if you just need to get away from Doo awhile? Don't you want to be able to do that?"

She touched my arm.

"Sometimes you just need to get in the car, roll down the window, and go for a ride. Turn on the radio and clear your head. Loretta, women have been driving for years. Get with the times. It's not that hard."

She was right and I knew it. I was twenty-nine years old with four kids. How could I not know how to drive a car? I really never thought too much about it before. Doo would always take me where we needed to go. I started thinking she was right. Why didn't I know how to drive? Was I that far behind in the times?

I nodded. I was in.

"Good! I thought you'd see it my way," she said. "Let me get my keys. I'll teach you right now. It'll be fun! We'll go slow and just drive down the street and back. Now don't look so worried," she said, then laughed. "I will be right there with you the whole time."

Patsy could talk anybody into anything. I told her once she could talk a sinner into a saint or a saint into a sinner.

You know how you start picturing yourself doing something you've never done before? Well, right then I started seeing myself jumping in the car anytime I wanted to. I could go to the grocery store instead of waiting for Doo to take me. Or I could go shopping for the kids. Heck, I could go shopping for myself!

Before I had even sat my rear end behind the wheel of a car, in my mind I was daydreaming about driving all over Nashville. An independent woman. Stranded no more! Heck, I was ten feet tall and bulletproof! Patsy was smiling that big full-face smile she had. She knew she had talked me into it.

Together we walked outside to her car. She opened the driver's-side door and said, "Now get in, Loretta." It felt funny to sit behind the wheel of a car. Strange, but also good. I put my hands on the steering wheel. I could already imagine the wind blowin' my hair!

Patsy walked around to the passenger side and jumped in. She handed me the keys and said, "Put your foot on the brake—yep, that's the one. Now start the car."

I froze. My leg started shaking so bad. I was vibrating the whole car. I must have turned pasty white, because Patsy started laughing so hard. She hollered, "Damn, Loretta, you ain't even started the car yet!" She usually talked so slick but with me sometimes her country would come out.

"Patsy," I said. "I think I may be sick. I am scared to death."

"Lord, Loretta, you are gonna be just fine. Now turn on the car."

I did just what she said.

"Car started, check! Now, put it in reverse."

"What's reverse?" I said.

She could see she had a lot to teach me then. "Keep your foot on the brake, now, honey. Here's what you do. Take the handle of the gear shift—that's the long handle there on the column. Now move it to over to 'R' for 'reverse,' so we can back out of the driveway."

Again I froze. What in the world? Patsy must have gotten frustrated with me, 'cause she said, "Hold on a minute." She got out and we changed places. She said, "I'll just back us out of the driveway. We will save 'reverse' for later."

When she had us pointed straight down her little street, we changed places again. You've probably seen movies where someone tries to teach someone to drive that cain't. Well, that was me. I am laughing even now, just thinking back on that day. I can hear Patsy so loud in my mind saying, "Gas! Brake! Gas! Brake! Less gas. Slow down! Stop!" Poor Patsy said I was making her a nervous wreck. By the time we got back to her house she was as white as I had been at the start. I guess she thought I was a lost cause because she never had me drive her car again. Maybe she thought she was doing the world a favor by keepin' me out from behind the wheel.

A year or so later Teddy and Doyle Wilburn taught me to drive. Doo never would ride with me. He said I drove too fast. But then, I am the only one in my family that has never gotten a speeding ticket, so there.

I think Patsy'd be proud.

Turning Up the Heat

In Nashville in 1962, we'd never heard of "feminism." It wasn't a thing yet, I don't reckon. And the sexual revolution sure hadn't hit Nashville. If it had, I sure hadn't heard of it. Either way, when me and Patsy met, I had been married to Doolittle Lynn for maybe fifteen years. I had four babies already. But I had never in my life had a climax.

I can't believe I am telling this, but I am. It's the truth and it's important. Y'all know me. I can't help but say the truth.

I honestly didn't know what a climax was. Therefore I didn't know what I wasn't having. Shoot, I never even heard the word before. Now I know I was not the only woman in the world who didn't know about orgasms until later in life, but still. I feel funny saying that word, *climax*. Or *orgasms*. But again, girls, it's important we know about these things. I didn't know what I was missing.

Now, don't get me wrong, I enjoyed sex. I mean, it may have not been my favorite thing to do. But I loved my husband. I wanted to be a good wife. Doo liked making love, but for me it was just okay. I would tell myself this is all part of being a good wife, right? Hey, it kept Doolittle happy. The way I saw it, it seemed to just keep me pregnant! Lots of times it would feel nice, but I just didn't see what all the fuss was about.

This was long before we had birth control pills. Shoot, if I had the pill I would have been taking it. (Like I told that *People* magazine, If I'd known, I'd have eaten 'em like popcorn.)

Growing up, we didn't talk about anything that had to do with your body—not about where babies came from or what a man and a woman do when they get married. Daddy said he got us babies from the cabbage patch. My parents said they didn't want me goin' 'round with Doo because he was "fast," but I thought that's because he had a Jeep. When they didn't want me getting married after a month of goin' with Doo, there weren't no birds-and-the-bees talk, I just thought they didn't want me leaving. They didn't talk about things like that. That's the way hill people were. The subject of sex was like a secret nobody was supposed to tell.

I was around thirteen when I had my first period. I had no idea what the heck was happening to me. I thought, *Oh my God, I am dying. I am bleeding to death!* I was so afraid. I didn't want to tell Mommy, but I had to. She looked at me a little sad when I told her. She had me follow her to her bedroom and she took out a little wicker sewing box. We sat there on her bed and she said, "Here." She handed me some cloth strips, like cut-up old bedsheets.

She told me about what she called a girl's "bleeding." She said, "Fold these and put them in your panties, Loretty. Change them every time you go potty." Then she dropped the big surprise. She said, "You're gonna have go through this once a month." I thought, *Are you kidding me?* She wasn't. Mommy said I'd become a woman. I weren't a girl no more. In my mind, that's why her face looked sad. I'd been Daddy's little girl. Now I guessed I couldn't be that anymore.

All of that made me feel dirty. It was messy. And it was painful. I'd curl up as tight as I could in a ball in my little bed from cramps. They'd last a couple of days, then the cramps would ease up. I told Marie Castle about my bleeding. She was my best childhood friend, remember? I felt like it was my job to tell her all about this woman stuff. Thinking back, I may have went a tad overboard—maybe stretched the truth about how bad it was. I liked to scare the heck out of Marie. A few days later my mommy called me in the house. She said, "Loretty, what in the fire did you say to little Marie about your bleeding?" Marie's mommy had told Mommy that I had scared Marie to death. I just thought Marie ought to know what was coming her way.

That's how I was when I met Doolittle. I didn't know much about the ways of the world. Hadn't dated or even kissed a boy. The only other boyfriend I ever had was Granvel Bolden, and we were just kids who would hold hands. And I would yell all over the playground, "I love Granvel Bolden." We'd write all over the schoolhouse

"LW + GB." One time I did get to go to the movies with him down in Paintsville, Kentucky. This was a big deal back then. I was so excited. I had never been to the movies before. We had to catch a bus in upper Van Lear, Kentucky, to take us to Paintsville to the Zip Movie Theater. Back then all them buses looked to me like the yellow school buses. The only reason Mommy let me go was because my brother Junior and his girlfriend Bonnie Faye were going. Mommy told Junior to watch after me. She knew Junior would.

It was late fall of 1947 when I met Doolittle Lynn. The first time I ever saw him, he'd just got back from the army, where he was stationed in Germany fighting in World War II. He'd come to our little one-room schoolhouse for our pie social. Doo was the auctioneer. I'll never forget it. He wore his army uniform. I swear he looked just like a little toy soldier. All us older girls at the school'd made pies. Those pies were auctioned off. Whichever boy bid the highest price on a girl's pie not only got the pie to eat, but he also got to walk that girl home. Well, I'd never made a pie before but I figured, how hard could it be? I made a chocolate pie. Mommy helped me with the crust and wrote down what I needed to do to cook the filling. I did the filling myself. I was so proud of that pie. It looked so pretty.

Doo paid five dollars for it—that was a lot of money back then. Doo sat down with that pie right next to me. When he bit into it, why, he liked to spit. I'd made that pie using salt instead of sugar! What did I know? I hadn't learned to cook yet.

Later, when Doo walked me home, he said, "Hey Loretta, how about a good night kiss?" I looked away. I was so shy. "Come on, Loretta," he said. "Ain't you ever been kissed before?" I hadn't, but didn't have a chance to tell him that. He just up and kissed me. He kissed me so hard! I said, "Oh, my, Doo. I can't breathe. I can't catch my breath." Doolittle said, "That's how you're supposed to feel when you're in love." I'd never been in love so when he told me that, I thought, *Well, heck, I guess I am in love.* Right then and there me and Doo started courting.

Daddy and Mommy didn't like Doo much. For one thing, Daddy said, Doo was too old for me. And plus he was wild as a buck. Both was true, I guess. Doo was seven years older than me. He'd been around.

But Doo was my first real boyfriend. My first kiss. My first everything.

The worst night of my life was our wedding night. It's sad to say, but it's true. I didn't know what to think when Doo wanted to make love. I ain't never heard of anybody doin' anything like that before. But Doo said all married people did it. All I knew was it made me feel shameful. You got to remember, I was just a girl, really.

Moving to Washington state was a good thing for our relationship—it made us rely on each other. If I'd have been closer to home, I'd have run back to my family. But living in Washington state, I couldn't do that. Doo loved me. I know that. But we had those babies so close together and we sure never had what you'd really call a honeymoon stage.

Which brings me back to what I was sayin' about my first climax.

Patsy and Charlie had no problem with showing each other affection in public. They were always hugging or kissing one another. Anybody could see how much Charlie loved Patsy. He'd watch her walk, just a-smilin'. He'd stare at her sometimes with this look. Patsy knew Charlie was watching her, too. She'd add a little more sway to her hips on purpose.

One day I said, "I wished Doolittle would love on me like Charlie does you, Patsy."

Patsy said, "Well, hell, Loretta, you got to give him a reason to. Spice things up."

"Spice things up like how?"

"Doo is a man and you're his woman. You gotta make him want to put his hands all over you."

I felt my face turn red, like I had a sunburn. Patsy said, "How long have you and Doo been married?" I told her.

"Fifteen years with the same woman?" I laughed at that. Doo may have been my only love, but I knew I wasn't his.

Patsy told me to follow her to her room. She said, "Honey, I'm going give you something that will turn Doolittle Lynn's head a-spinning."

Patsy opened a drawer and started pulling out all kinds of sexy bras and little lace nighties. I swear she had a drawerful. Finally she said, "Here, Little Gal. This one's perfect for you." She smiled. "It matches the color of your cheeks." She tossed me a tiny see-through red lace nightie.

I had never seen anything like it. I swear it looked like it was just a strip of lace.

"Now how on earth am I gonna sleep in this thing?" I asked.

Patsy 'bout died laughing. She said, "I don't think you will be getting much sleep in that little number!" That day Patsy gave me a whole boxful of clothes, plus a couple of nighties and lacy panties to wear. She knew I didn't have anything like that. When I got home I just put it all away in my dresser. I had no plans of wearing lacy underwear. I could not even imagine myself in them. You hear women talk about being sexy or feeling sexy nowadays. I hardly knew what those words meant!

It was some time later Doo and I got into a bad argument about something or another. Doolittle huffed and growled out of the house, as usual. I was tired of him just huffing off like that. He was gone for a long time, but that night was different. Instead of me just going to bed and falling asleep, I thought about what Patsy had said. Right then, I decided I wasn't some little wife who was gonna sit around and wait for their man to come home anymore. I was gonna really make him think about what he had. I'd take Patsy's advice. I'd stay up and wait for him. I took a nice long bath and I dug out a pair of those lacy panties Patsy gave me. I only owned two cotton nightgowns—one was the one Doo's momma gave me for our honeymoon. So this was a big deal to me. With the kids sleeping, I fixed my hair, put on just a little rouge to brighten up my cheeks and lips, and slipped into that sexy pair of panties. Now, friends, I had never really looked at my body before, I mean really looked. With those panties on, I stood frozen at the mirror just staring at myself. I looked good—sexy, even. It felt strange seeing myself like that. But it felt right powerful, too. I had never thought of myself as sexy in any way. Sure, I worried about Doo stepping out with other women, but when it came to me, I hardly thought about sex at all. Seemed like when I looked at the mirror that night, looking back at me wasn't a shy girl. What I saw was a grown woman. And I liked her.

When Doo finally got home I was ready for him in the nightie and panties. He walked through the bedroom door hollerin', "Loretta, why is the light still on? Why aren't you in bed?" And then he saw me. I will never forget the look on his face. Right then and there I knew what Patsy meant. Doo's head was a-spinning, in a good way. In all our years together Doo had never looked at me like that. Like he couldn't get enough, staring like he was gonna eat me up.

Patsy was right about not sleeping, too. We didn't do much sleeping at all. I can't explain the way it made me feel to just know I was so wanted and loved. And I wasn't afraid to tell Doo what felt good and ask for more. Like I said, I felt strong. That night I had my very first climax. It kinda scared me at first. I didn't know what was happening, I just knew it felt different and good. I told Doolittle something happened and I explained what I had felt to him. He just said, "That's great, honey."

The next day Doo and I were like lovebirds. We wanted

each other. We started enjoying being together. And I was a quick learner. I became a little braver, bolder. That feelin' made a difference. It changed me in other ways—like how I sang and what I wrote. Like "To Make a Man Feel Like a Man." I never thought a lot about that before, even after I'd been married a long time. Now here I was, singing, "You gotta show him you are a woman." Writing helped me work through things like that. It helped me make sense of it somehow.

I really started to like the new, improved Loretta. When we got a few extra dollars, I'd buy a sexy pair of panties just for me and Doo. He loved it.

Maybe I was a late bloomer. I don't care. I'm just thankful I had a girlfriend who embraced me for who I was and helped me out. For Patsy they were just sexy nighties or panties. To me, her gift was so much more. It was like she gave me my real first step into womanhood.

I kept one of the nighties Patsy gave me. The red one. It's in my museum at my ranch along with some of the other things she gave me. Each one has a special meaning to me. That red nightie? Well, I have to smile every time I see it. Patsy, you were right. It matches the color of my cheeks.

Vegas Headliner

In the fall of 1962, when the DJs gathered in Nashville for the Country Music Awards, Patsy was ready. For the awards ceremony, she pulled out all the stops. The reigning Queen of Country Music wore a gold brocade dress, gold heels—even a tiara. She looked like the queen she was.

Again, the country music DJs voted Patsy their Favorite Female Artist. And the awards kept her on her feet—this year without crutches. Amid all the congratulations, she said, "It's wonderful, but what am I gonna do for 1963? It's getting so even the Cline can't follow the Cline!"

After the awards show, while Patsy was busy talking with reporters, Randy negotiated a big surprise for her. He'd booked her for an unprecedented gig. Headlining in Las Vegas!

Patsy was impressed. The biggest superstars played Las Vegas, people like Sinatra and Elvis. They didn't ask country music stars to play Vegas, except maybe somebody huge like Johnny Cash, so this was pretty special. And, besides that, it was pretty unheard of for a woman to headline there.

Besides, the money would be good. Randy negotiated six thousand dollars a week!

When she told me the news, I was almost more excited than she was! But the more I thought about it, the more I started to worry. Was Patsy well enough for such a demanding gig? She still wore headbands to help ease her ongoing headaches. Sometimes she got to hurting so bad the only thing that helped was resting her head on the cold tile in her bathroom. She said she was up to it, so I shut my big mouth.

Patsy decided to ramp up her wardrobe for the trip. She said, "This is Vegas, Little Gal!" She ordered several sleek new gowns and pretty shoes. My favorite was a long white chiffon gown. It was gorgeous, with a long, full skirt and a sequined top. She carried on over it something fierce. She hired a choreographer, too, and worked out a real professional routine. She wanted it to be a real classy act.

As the date neared, Patsy got more and more nervous. It was such late notice they had trouble finding musicians to back her. Then Randy found the Glaser Brothers, who backed up Roy Orbison. She'd worked with them before. The bad news was they wouldn't rehearse. They said it wasn't in their contract. I knew it'd be fine. She had a way of leading whatever musicians she played with. She wasn't one to just stand out in front and sing.

The Wilburn Brothers and me had played a show there that fall, so she asked Teddy for advice. He told her not to worry. They could rehearse in some of the big rooms they had there in the hotel. That calmed her down some.

Patsy opened on November 23. She played seven nights a week for five weeks. It was grueling. Performing in Vegas is a lot different than playing the Grand Ole Opry, where the whole place loves you. For one thing, Patsy had to perform at what's called a dinner show. Folks are eating while you're up there singing your heart out, and they're more interested in their steaks than in you. A lot of the people there are seeing the show for free because the casinos give out tickets to high rollers and VIPs. Patsy said the whole place was filled with mobsters. She could've been a-fibbing about the mobsters, but most likely she wasn't.

She came down with "Vegas throat." Her throat was parched from that dry, desert air, so she had to lip-sync. She hated to do it, but what choice was there? Poor Patsy was racked with regret. Still, there wasn't anything she could do about it. She had to suck it up and keep performing, like she'd always done.

Talk about homesick. Every chance she got, Patsy called family and friends back home. She had always talked about how it was getting harder and harder to leave her babies. She'd say, "My babies are getting old enough to miss me." So all she could think about was making it back to celebrate Christmas with the kids. But then a few days before they were supposed to leave, Randy booked her at another hotel! Patsy was furious. This only added to how bad she felt about having to be gone for so long.

After she got home, she said she didn't know if she'd

ever leave again. "I wanna slow down. No matter what, I'm never gonna do this again," she said. But we all knew she'd be back at it soon. Patsy loved performing and she loved her fans. And she liked being successful, earning top dollar for her performances at last.

From then on, she called Nella Drive "the House That Vegas Built."

Happy Anniversary to Me

On January 10, 1963, I woke up thinking about my wedding day. Fifteen years before that, me and Doolittle were standin' there in that little courthouse, with my daddy silent behind us. Seemed like a lifetime ago. It felt like me and Doo'd been together forever. We were both so young when we married! I went straight from my daddy's lap into my husband's arms. Hell, I was just a girl then, and here I was now, a momma of four with a career in country music, livin' in Nashville, Tennessee.

Me and Doo'd been through so much—hard times and good ones. We'd stayed together and ridden out a lot of storms. I guess I felt like maybe we really had made it. Our kids were growing up and had begun taking some care of themselves. We started doing things, just him and me. We'd go to friends' or just take a ride somewhere and not have to worry about them too much. It was good. The kids were adjusting to living in Nashville, too. They'd started school and were making new friends. They seemed happy. Add to that, for the first time in our marriage we finally had a little money. We were able to buy the kids bikes. They had some toys and more than one change of clothes. I never could have imagined what we had here back when we lived in Washington state. Career-wise I was making some headway. I'd been charting singles and selling records, touring. And there was whispers I was being considered for the Most Promising Female Country Singer. Doo liked his job. We were getting along good, too. We hardly ever fussed anymore, and when we did it weren't over anything big. Things were looking up. It seemed like smooth sailing for once in our lives.

'Course our anniversary wasn't something we ever really made a big deal about before. We never had the time or money to think much about it, I guess. It was a kiss and a hug, or Doo might give me a card sometime. I wasn't expecting this year to be much different. Why should I? I was okay with that. What mattered was that we were happy, really happy, for the first time in a long time.

When I got up that morning, Doolittle'd already left for work. So I got the kids up and ready for school. My favorite time of the morning was right after they caught the bus. I'd make me a cup of coffee and sit at the kitchen table and look at the paper. I always had a pencil and something to write on. You wouldn't believe how inspired I could get reading a newspaper. President John F. Kennedy was changing the world. There was usually news about the progress he was making. I liked looking at the pictures in the newspaper, too. Still do. Back then, there were grainy black-and-white pictures and they always drew me in. There was something so truthful about them. I'd look through the paper and write down any ideas or phrases that I could use in a song somewhere. I'd do that and drink my coffee and think about the day.

I remember I laid out some chicken to thaw for supper and started cleaning up the dirty dishes, makin' beds—just daily routine stuff. Then the doorbell rang. Patsy and Dottie West had stopped by for a minute. Dottie'd brought me a beautiful new embroidered tablecloth. It was so nice! It was made from real fancy material. It had gold leaves woven into the cream cloth. I loved it. I thanked her and said I couldn't wait to use it for nice dinners. It was so sweet of her. Having nice things was still new to me. That gift made me feel really special.

Then Patsy said, "Happy anniversary! Fifteen years, right? What are you and Doo's plans for tonight?"

"Yep, fifteen," I said. "Plans? Why, I'm not sure, really."

Dottie, who was always funny and really quick-witted, said, "Loretta, you deserve a big steak dinner and a crown! One like they give out in beauty pageants for staying married that long and raising all your kids."

Patsy laughed. "Yep," she said. "Especially for stayin' with Mooney Lynn!"

I laughed right along with the girls. But I started feeling bad that we didn't have plans. Maybe in Nashville folks made a big deal out of anniversaries. I didn't really know. Suddenly I found myself saying, "Y'all know Doo. He won't tell me nothing. He probably made some big surprise plan for us tonight."

Patsy said, "You better wear something sexy tonight!" They both teased me until my cheeks turned red.

After the girls left, Teddy Wilburn came to pick me up. We went over to the Wil-Helm office and spent most of the day writing like we did whenever we weren't on the road. Then Teddy started in on me about me and Doo's anniversary. "Got some big plans tonight, Loretta? Where's Doo taking you? Did he get you some flowers?" I almost laughed. I thought, *Doo, buy flowers? Are you kiddin'?* My husband was more the type to bring home a slab of a cow. He'd say, "Here, baby, look what I got you!" But I couldn't say that. So I just stuck with the story I'd told the girls earlier—that Doo was probably cookin' up a surprise. Teddy said, "Good for Mooney. I'm sure he has something great planned."

Wasn't long before I found myself getting mad at Doolittle. I'd started the day happy, and now I was feelin' hurt. Doo hadn't planned a dadgum thing for us and I just knew it. He'd come home dirty from work like every night before, hungry and expecting me to have dinner ready. Maybe, if I was lucky, he might say, "Happy anniversary, baby." And honestly we'd never celebrated before. So why was I not okay with that now? Why had I worked myself up so bad? Maybe it was because I lied to everyone. Or maybe I was upset because what I wished would happen wouldn't—and I knew it.

By the time Teddy dropped me back home I was really mad—hurt, angry, you name it. I was callin' Doo every name I could think of inside my head. I went through every bad thing that Doo had done for the last fifteen years. I remember we had this mirror on the wall right as you opened the front door to the house. After Teddy pulled out of the drive, I walked up to that mirror. I said, "You're the dummy, Loretta! Putting up with all Doo's crap for years!" I hollered at my reflection. Then I heard my oldest daughter coming around the corner, walkin' in, real careful. She said, "Momma, you okay?" I couldn't help it. I know it was wrong to say, but I couldn't hold back anymore. I said, "I am fine, Betty Sue, but your daddy won't be if he forgets it's our anniversary tonight."

Betty Sue looked confused. She said, "Your what?"

Right then I thought, *My Lord, even our own children don't know that these dates are important. What kind of parents are we?*

When Doolittle came home that night, I had dinner ready on the stove. And, of course, I'd been right—he didn't have anything planned for us. It was just an ordinary night to him. There he was, wearin' his dirty work clothes, waiting on me to fix his plate of dinner—of course! Just like I thought he'd be. I was so upset I could spit.

Doo knew something was wrong. He knew me better 'n' anybody. He said, "Baby, you okay?"

"I guess," I said.

"Something happen today? You look like you're about to shoot somebody."

I whirled around on him so fast! "What is today?" I said, all fired up.

Doo looked shocked. So I asked again, "What is today?"

You shoulda seen the look on Doo's face. It was like he was a little scared of me. "Must be Loretta Has Lost Her Mind Day," he said. "Hell! I don't know, Loretta. What is today?"

"It's our fifteenth anniversary, Doo!" I said.

Doo got right up from the table and strolled over to me. He kissed me on the cheek and said, "I'm sorry, baby. Happy anniversary." Then he went back and sat down, ready to eat.

That did it. I could feel myself gettin' hotter and hotter. I had a bowl of beans in my hands I was about to dish out. I promise I didn't plan what came next. I just did it. I took that bowl of beans over to Doo and dumped the whole bowl over his head. He was covered in beans and juice. He stood up so fast his chair went a-flying. I thought, *You've really done it this time, Loretta.* For a second I thought Doo was gonna hit me. He reared back with his hand raised like he was gonna. The kids heard the noise from that chair, I guess, because they came running in the kitchen to see what the heck was going on. When Jack Benny saw his daddy covered in beans, he started laughing. Then Ernest Ray and Cissie started laughing, too. Poor Doo.

Doo started yelling at me and at the kids. He stormed out of the house, still covered in beans. I heard him get into the car and leave.

I was glad to see him go. I knew I'd went too far. We both needed to cool off.

So me and the kids got busy cleaning up the kitchen. Little Cissie was worried about her daddy. She started crying. She said, "Why did you pour beans on Daddy?"

"Oh, honey," I said. "I didn't mean to." I lied and said I'd tripped and those beans flew out of my hands. How could I tell her the truth? *I* didn't even know why I did it! Betty Sue was just starting those awful teenage years. She piped up and said, "Sure you did, Momma. You tripped and them beans landed right on top of Daddy's head." She gave me a look like, *Nice try, Momma.*

Now this was the first time I ever dumped a bowl of beans on Doolittle Lynn, but it wouldn't be the last. They became my weapon of choice. If beans was around when I got good and mad, you can bet he'd run.

That night I waited and waited, but Doolittle didn't come home. He stayed out all night long. I tell you, I was worried sick. I was upset before, but now I was really worried.

Doo finally come home the next morning. He still had on his work clothes and he still had beans in his hair and on his clothes. I just up and started with, "I am so sorry, honey. I swear I don't know what happened. I think I went a little crazy." *That's it, Loretta*, I said to myself. *You've just been working too hard.*

Doo never moved. He had propped himself against the bedroom door and stood there looking at me. He said, "Why didn't you tell me you wanted me to take you somewhere and celebrate our anniversary? All you had to do was ask."

I went over to hug Doo. I said, "I don't want to ask. I wanted to be asked." He looked me right in the eye and said, "But, honey, I didn't know that." I said, "What? You can't read my mind?" We both smiled at that. Then Doo, dirty shirt, dried bean juice all over him, kissed me. I mean he really kissed me.

Doolittle didn't go to work that day. He called and told them he was taking off the day to spend it with his wife. We even took a bath together. We had never done that before. Our tub wasn't built for two people, but it didn't matter—it was nice. We spent most of the day in bed, just the two of us. I was in such bliss. We may have missed out on celebrating the day before, but our anniversary got celebrated just the same.

I was so happy.

And then it hit me. My DIAPHRAGM! In all the drama, I'd forgotten to wear my diaphragm. Are you kidding me? No! Folks, this was long before birth control pills.

I was like a cat on a hot tin roof carrying on. "Doolittle!" I said, "I forgot my diaphragm! What are we gonna do? Oh my gosh, I can't be having no baby!"

Doo said to calm down. He thought I was overreacting. "You don't get pregnant every time you have sex, Loretta. It's gonna be okay. Besides, what's the big deal if you had another baby, anyway?" I looked at Doo and I could see he meant it. He wouldn't mind at all if we had four kids or twenty. Suddenly, he looked so hurt. "Loretta, don't you want any more of my babies?" He had tears starting up in his baby-blue eyes—those eyes I loved so much. I never wanted to hurt him.

But the truth was, I didn't. I honestly didn't want any more babies—not at this point in my life, just when things were starting to be okay. But I couldn't say no. I couldn't tell Doo that after all those years of feeling stuck at home with the kids, just wondering when and if Doo would come home, finally, finally, I had a little bit of a life of my own. I loved Doo, but I didn't want to go backward. Not yet, when success was so close. So I just said, "We have enough going on without another baby. Let's just hope we got lucky this time." I grabbed my housecoat and headed into the bathroom. I closed the door and prayed. I said, "Lord, please! I do not want another baby. Not now. Please!"

A few weeks later, sure enough, I found out I was pregnant. *Damn it*, I thought. *I am the unluckiest woman in the world.* I didn't tell a soul. Not Doo. No one. Patsy was out of town and I wanted to talk to her first. That was the longest week of my life.

Finally, a Day Off

It was a cold day in early January when me and Patsy finally had a day off together. She'd been in some kind of big fight with Charlie. I came over to her house and she blew off some steam, cussing him and ranting for a while. Finally I said, "So I guess you're leaving him, then, huh?" She looked at me then and I looked at her and we both stared a minute. Then we both just busted out laughing. We laughed 'til we cried.

She said, "How about you and me head into town instead?"

Patsy had just given away her cowgirl stage outfits to Pearl Butler. That country western look was behind her now, and she said she wouldn't need them anymore. So we went into Nashville to pick up some new dresses she'd ordered. They were beautiful. One was a long-sleeved white dress. I thought it was about the prettiest thing I'd ever seen. When she tried it on, I told her the truth: She looked like an angel.

That whole day I felt like blurting out, "Patsy, I think

I'm pregnant!" But I didn't. I felt like once I did, it'd be true. So we talked about everything else.

Patsy could tell something was off with me. Finally, when we got back to her house, she said, "What's up with you, Little Gal? Something's off."

That's when I told her. "I think I'm pregnant!"

"Oh, Loretta! That's great!" When she went to hug me, I started crying.

"It's not great! I don't want another baby right now."

Patsy hugged me. She rocked me and assured me it would all be okay.

"Come on now, Little Gal," she said. "God don't give us more than we can bear. Besides, it'd be nice to have another little one running around. In fact"—she got up then and started poking around in her closet—"I still have some of my maternity clothes! Things I wore when I was pregnant with Randy. I'll gather them up for you, how about that? You're gonna love this jacket I got. It's flashy gold—great for the stage. It can hide your belly for months!"

Now, remember: No working country artists back then took along their kids on the road. That wasn't even considered. And we didn't have nannies to look after our kids at home. Still, Patsy had two little kids. She toured and made hit records. She was a loving momma, and her kids were happy and healthy. Was it a good time for me to have a baby? No. But if Patsy could do it, maybe so could I.

Patsy took me by the hand and said, "Now, Loretta, you

do what's best for you. I'll be right with you, no matter what."

I understood what she was saying. It was like she'd always taught me: It was my body and my life. Nobody could or should make choices for me. I looked at that box of maternity clothes, at the gold jacket that could hide any baby bump. I knew right then I'd be able to do it. I could perform and still be a good momma.

I could do this.

A few weeks later I miscarried. It surprised me how sad that made me. I'd been all worked up worrying I was gonna have another baby, then I was disappointed when I wasn't. The good thing about it was, I figured out I could handle pretty much whatever was around the bend. Patsy taught me that.

The Last Recording Session

In early February 1963, Patsy went back in the studio for an album Owen was putting together. They recorded several oldies like "Blue Moon of Kentucky," "Always," and "Sweet Dreams."

Patsy was real emotional, crying on nearly every take. You can hear her voice break on "Faded Love." Some singers today will fake that, but that really was Patsy crying. She just felt everything so deeply.

Patsy truly loved traditional country music, and she was over the moon recording this album. She was singing a lot of her favorite songs. But the money was in the crossover sound that Patsy and Owen now had down to a fine art. For this record, Owen's arrangements were even more elaborate and lush. He'd brought in a small orchestra, plus the Jordanaires for backup. This time Patsy wasn't worried about that. She'd proved Patsy Cline couldn't be crowded out.

Recording that album could not have come at a better time for Patsy because she could forget her troubles on the home front for a while. But only for a while. I can't tell you exactly what was happening with Patsy and Charlie—maybe it was his drinking, maybe it was her being gone so much, I just don't know. All I can say is that around this time they were in real trouble, like D-I-V-O-R-C-E trouble. I wish she would have talked to me more about what was going on with them, but she was so dadgum proud and stubborn. If I had known how bad it was, I would have dropped everything to be there for her in a second. But Patsy never said a word and Charlie didn't, neither.

I heard Charlie Dick showed up at the studio while Patsy was recording, upset and wanting to talk to her. Owen told him to leave and he did. Again, I never saw Charlie hit Patsy, but whatever happened, I do now know that Charlie was thrown in jail for whipping Patsy pretty bad. Bad enough that Dottie said Patsy filed for divorce.

A lot of y'all may wonder how the heck I wouldn't have known about the troubles with Charlie and Patsy. At that time I was starting my first big tour with Teddy and Doyle Wilburn. For weeks, I had been over the moon about the chance to perform with the boys on the road, and we had been practicing nonstop. I really think Patsy didn't want to worry me with her problems. She was like that. She never wanted to lay her troubles on anyone. I have to believe she thought this was just another way of loving and protecting me. If it wasn't for our friend Dottie West telling me months later, I would never have believed it.

By the time I returned from our tour, Patsy and Charlie seemed to have worked things out. For a long time I was secretly really upset at Patsy, like she didn't trust me enough. Did she feel like she could not talk to me about something so bad? I didn't know, but if she wasn't sharing, I wasn't pushing. Marriage is not a group affair. The worst troubles Doo and I ever had was when we had others picking sides. Still, I can't even imagine how Charlie could do that to Patsy. Doolittle and I may have had fights, but, friends, Doo never beat me up. I have always said Doo never gave me anything I didn't give him back double. He would have never taken a fist to me—never! Later, I found it in my heart to forgive Charlie. I know how much he loved his wife and the kids. Charlie and I never spoke about that incident. I always have said it's not our job to judge. I would never want that job.

The last day of recording, Owen was playing back the finished tracks for Patsy. It was a little listening party, and everybody was ready to celebrate. Patsy went next door to the office and found a copy of her first single, "A Church, a Courtroom, and Then Goodbye." She held it high and said, "Here you have it, folks! The first record and the last!"

That got Jan Howard upset. "Patsy!" she hollered. "Don't say that!"

Patsy shrugged it off like she was just talking about the way the records sounded so different—a sort of before-and-after thing. I'm not so sure. I think Patsy knew she'd recorded her final record.

Last Day Together

For years, me and Doo had dreamed of having a little piece of land all our own. So after "Success," we finally had a little money. We moved out of that rental home into a place we'd bought in Goodlettsville, just north of Nashville.

Out there we had plenty of room to roam. I may have worn the cowgirl outfits back when I started out, but Doo was the real cowboy. He didn't just wear the hat, either. He had competed in rodeos when he was younger and it was always kind of in his blood. He had this idea that we could put on rodeos where I could perform right there in our own backyard. He was just clever enough and bullheaded enough to make most of those dreams happen, too. We did it! And after a few years our rodeo got so big we had to take it to the Nashville Fairgrounds. But that would come later.

That Thursday, February 28, 1963, we were still moving in. Patsy surprised me at the new house. As a house-warming gift, she'd had her seamstress make me some new drapes, just like hers in the House That Vegas Built, plus a couple of ottomans. That day she helped me hang the curtains. It was her and me standing on chairs with pins in our mouths—real elegant! I remember we talked about her plans for the kids' rooms. She couldn't stay long after that, but promised to call later.

That night, me and Doo were wiped out from working on that new house. We fell into bed early, but then Patsy called. Owen had sent over the session tapes for her new album. She said, "Y'all get your butts out of bed and come on over here to the house. We're gonna have us a little listening party right here in the music room."

She didn't have to ask twice. We drove on over. We came in through the music-room door and I remember little Randy was still awake, rocking on this little horse he'd got for Christmas.

"All right now," Patsy said. "Listen up and tell me what you think."

Patsy sat with us downstairs while we listened, embroidering a tablecloth. I couldn't believe this superstar with a voice for the ages was sitting there sewing with a needle and thread.

After a while, Patsy said, "So, what do you think? Am I going too far away from country music?"

Friends, this was a big concern for Patsy. She never wanted to lose her country roots. She trusted me and she valued my opinion, so she looked at me dead center in the eyes and said, "Loretta, tell me the truth. Do you think I am? Do you think my fans will like these songs?"

I looked at her straight back into her eyes, "Patsy, this whole dang record is a hit. Every last song on it is great." And I meant every word of it, too. Sitting there, hearing Patsy sing "She's Got You," was unforgettable. That's a memory I hold so close.

"It don't get no better than this, Patsy. This record is perfect. I love it."

That seemed to please her.

Patsy had back-to-back trips planned for that weekend—Birmingham and then Kansas.

She offered me seventy dollars to come and sing that weekend. Her manager, Randy, had his pilot's license and a little yellow plane. I never flew in it—Faron called it a "shit box"—but Patsy wasn't a bit afraid. She'd ride with Randy to dates here and there, even sometimes just for fun.

"Come on, Loretta. Randy will fly us. It'll be fun!"

I couldn't. The boys had booked me for a gig at a place in Memphis. I hated to say no—it seemed like Patsy didn't want to go alone. But I couldn't back out of the Memphis deal. She understood that well enough.

It was getting real late. As usual, Patsy wanted to send me home with something. She ran upstairs and came back with a box of clothes, along with some pretty, dangly earrings. We made plans to go shopping when she got back from Kansas City. Doo was tired and ready to get home and back in bed, so I was heading out with him when suddenly I stopped.

"Doo! I forgot to say good-bye to Patsy," I said. I set that box down on the hood of Charlie's Cadillac and ran back to hug her. That moment of running back to hug my friend one last time is one that I treasure. I believe with all my heart God stepped in there and led me back to give her that final hug. My last words to her were, "Patsy, I sure wish I could come with you." She said, "It's all right, Little Gal. Don't you worry. We're gonna stick together."

The Day Patsy Died

The winds were howling something fierce. I lay in my bed, listening, and the wind sounded just awful—mournful. Seemed like I heard a tune in that wind. I knew something bad was going on when I heard that. I could feel it—I just didn't know what it was. I listened hard. I tried to make out what the voices in the wind were saying. Later, thinking back, I wondered if maybe Patsy was singing to me in the wind.

That wasn't my first premonition. All mountain people are like that. My mommy had it. She knew things—not everything, but sometimes she'd know something before it happened. She could read coffee grounds and tea leaves. I have a little bit of that, too. I just feel things sometimes, or I dream 'em.

Like when my daddy died. Me and Doo was living in Washington state. One night I saw Daddy in my dream. He came to me, calling the name he used to call me when I was a girl. "Loretty," he said, real calm. He was wearing his dark blue suit and he waved at me. I could see him just as clear as day in my dream. I woke Doo up with all my tossin'. He said, "What is it, baby?"

I said, "It's Daddy. Something's wrong."

Doo said, "No, honey, your daddy's fine. Go back to sleep." But I just knew.

In the morning my landlady came over. She said, "Loretta, somebody's called on the phone and they want to talk to you." And sure enough. I answered that call and they told me. Daddy was gone.

Later, I told Mommy that story. Mommy wasn't surprised. She said he'd missed me so bad. I was his first girl and he never wanted me to leave home. He made Doo promise not to take me away when we got married, but he did. We can't always keep our promises, even if we want to and we try to. But I'd always been Daddy's girl, even two thousand miles away. He must have wanted to see me one last time before he passed over.

While I lay there listening to the wind howl in Nashville, Patsy was in Kansas, singing Hank Williams's song "I'll Sail My Ship Alone." When I heard that song later, it like to kill me, Patsy talking about giving a message to the wind, "hoping you would hear my S.O.S."

I finally fell asleep. I didn't think about it again 'til much later.

That weekend Randy flew Patsy to Birmingham, where she'd done three performances. It was only supposed to be two, but the concert promoter begged for a third and Patsy obliged. They flew back for the night, then Sunday morning they flew out again for Kansas City with Cowboy Copas and Hawkshaw Hawkins.

Patsy was in Kansas City for a benefit show. Like me,

she had a soft spot for country radio disc jockeys. So when George Jones called her to tell her about a benefit for "Cactus Jack" Call, who'd died in a car accident, she said yes. The memorial concert, arranged by Hap Peebles, was to raise money for Jack's family. Patsy's heart went out to Cactus Jack's family. She met his wife and two little sons that night. Knowing Patsy, she must have just loved on them kids.

Sunday night she closed the show. Dottie West watched Patsy perform in that gorgeous white gown we'd picked up in town. "She was just beautiful," Dottie said later. "It seemed she sang so effortlessly." The audience gave Patsy a standing ovation.

Patsy was exhausted after that. She called her momma on the phone and said she couldn't wait to get home and rest. She had a bad cold—maybe even the flu. There was an afterparty and they couldn't head back that night, so she and all the other performers stayed overnight in a hotel there in Kansas City. Patsy planned to get on back home with Randy in his plane the next morning.

The next morning she met the others for breakfast at the hotel, all of 'em talking about the rain. They'd have to wait for it to clear up to fly out. Dottie and her husband, Bill, had a car and asked Patsy to come back with them. But Patsy really wanted to get back to her babies. She figured flying would get her back sooner. Dottie was worried about her, flying in that bad weather. "Don't worry about me, Hoss," she said. "When it's my time to go, it's my time to go." What kind of a thing to say is that? I wonder sometimes, what if I had been with her? Could I have talked her into riding with Dottie?

Finally they got cleared to fly out. It was Randy, Patsy, Hawkshaw Hawkins, and Cowboy Copas. The weather was so bad Randy had to stop more than once. Their last stop was in Dyersburg, Tennessee, where they refueled and got some coffee. The airport manager offered to loan them his car to get home, but Randy said they'd be fine. After that, nobody heard from them. They sent out a search party. Turns out Randy'd crashed that plane in Camden, Tennessee—just ninety miles outside Nashville. Everybody on board died instantly.

I believe Patsy had a feeling she was going to die soon. She'd almost died as a child with rheumatic fever, then again in that car wreck. She'd told Ray Walker, "The third one'll either be the charm or kill me." She even wrote up a will on a Delta Airlines paper telling how little Julie and Randy ought to be raised. She said what she wanted to be buried in: a white dress she'd designed, wearing Julie's gold cross necklace and holding Randy's little white Bible. Plus she'd been giving away a bunch of her things before she died. Even for Patsy, who was generous like nobody I ever met, it was unusual. I think she knew.

I heard later that when rescuers found Patsy's wristwatch, it had stopped at 6:20 p.m. That was the moment my life as I knew it stopped. I couldn't imagine living without Patsy. But I was going to have to.

March Chills

There are certain dates in everyone's life that feel heavier than all the rest. Not the holidays or birthdays—I mean a day that means something just to you. Everybody else goes on about their business, but, for you, that date's like an alarm clock set to blast in your head and crack open your heart every damn year. One of those days for me is March 5. That's the day we lost Patsy Cline. I hate thinking about this loss still. It is as real and as raw to me today as the day it happened. Reliving all the times Patsy and I had together for this book has been good, but it's also reopened that feeling of empty sadness.

Me and Patsy had made plans to go shopping after she got back from Kansas City. We'd meant to go on Tuesday, but then she didn't get out on time 'cause of the weather. I got up real early Wednesday morning so I'd have time to get ready for our shopping trip. It was getting late, and I was just about to pick up the phone to call her. I was gonna say, "You lazy head, why ain't you here yet?" But before I could, the phone rang in my hand. I figured it was Patsy, but it was the booking agent for her show saying Patsy's plane had gone down.

I said, "Baloney, her and me's going shopping."

I hung up the phone and told Doo what I'd just heard. I refused to believe it. He turned on the radio. Then the news came on and we heard it for sure. Randy's plane had crashed. The pilot and three passengers were killed. When I heard those words—"no survivors"—I must've started hollering, telling Doo to take me quick to Patsy's house. Doo stopped me and said, "No, Loretta." I started hitting him, crying and yelling that it was a lie. I don't remember any of that. I don't remember anything. I was in shock.

We spent the day at Patsy's house. Charlie had brought her body home to her dream house, like she'd wanted. It was a tough day for everybody.

I'd lost the best friend I'd ever had. And it wasn't just my loss. The Nashville country music family lost four of its members, all in one fell swoop. We're a close-knit community, even today. You couldn't turn on a country music radio station without hearing one of their songs. Everyone was grieving.

The Thursday after the crash, there was a big prayer service at the Phillips-Robinson Funeral Home. The city shut down the streets because thousands of fans surrounded the place. The caskets were closed. They just had photos of Patsy, Cowboy Copas, Randy Hughes, and Hawkshaw Hawkins above their caskets. I'd never seen so many flowers. Thousands and thousands of 'em. You wouldn't believe it.

The funeral home was packed with friends and loved ones. Dottie West, Kitty Wells—all our friends were there. I sat down with Doo and Doyle Wilburn. I wasn't ready to say good-bye. I told Doo that morning I didn't want to go. But Doo said, "Baby, we have to go. We need to be there for Charlie and the kids." Doolittle always had such a big heart. At some point, a couple of policemen came in and spoke quietly to Kitty Wells and her husband, Johnnie Wright. Then we saw them get up and leave. I figured there was a parking issue or something, but come to find out Johnnie's singing partner, Jack Anglin, was killed in a car accident on the way to the memorial service. It was just too sad for words. Why was everybody dying?

Folks started to wonder if maybe the Grand Ole Opry was jinxed. I was pretty spooked, for sure. I couldn't hardly get in a car without getting nervous and shaky. Jack Anglin had died in that car accident on the way to the prayer service for Patsy and them. Then a bunch of other country music artists died while traveling over the next couple of years. Ernest and Jean Shepard were in a car wreck that year. Then Jim Reeves—he died in a car crash, too. Ira Louvin of the Louvin Brothers died in a car wreck. Our friend Roy Acuff was seriously injured in a car wreck, but he made it out alive. It was upsetting how many lives were torn apart just trying to get somewhere to perform. Looking back, I guess we all traveled so much it's a wonder it weren't worse.

We were all pretty spooked.

After Hilda took Patsy back to Winchester, Doo and me

went back over to Charlie's. Doo talked to him. I couldn't find the right words to say. My heart was breaking. So I just sat there in Patsy's house, remembering all the times we'd shared. All of a sudden a song took hold of me. The words and the melody came all in a rush. It took me about twenty minutes to get it down. That's when I wrote the lyrics to "This Haunted House." I played it for Charlie.

I watched you leave
that's how I know you're gone
But this heart of mine keeps telling me I'm wrong.

"I wrote it for you," I said. I asked what he thought. Tears rolled down his face. "It's beautiful," he said.

I recorded it later. That song's still real special to me.

I wanted so badly to do something, anything, to help Patsy's family, but Doo said I needed to give them space. This loss had hit Charlie really hard—harder than anybody knew. Hilda took Randy and Julie home with her for a while until he could get back on his feet.

I waited six full days to visit Charlie again, then I couldn't take it no more. I made a roast with potatoes, onions, and carrots, and Doo drove me over to the house. We knocked and knocked, but nobody came to the door. I knew full well Charlie was there. So I opened the door and let myself in. The place was a mess. I told Doo I wanted to clean it up. He should go on and come back for me later.

I found Charlie in the music room where we'd spent so many good times together. Charlie always liked to serve up drinks at the bar that said *Patsy and Charlie's* in red leather. Poor Charlie looked rough. He lay on the floor surrounded by beer cans. Trash was all over the place. He had a reel-to-reel player hooked up playin' Patsy's new album. When the tape ended, he scrambled over and run the tape back to listen again.

I didn't know what to do. Finally I laid down next to him on the floor. We listened to that album and cried together.

Finally Charlie said, "What in the hell am I gonna do now, Loretta?" I didn't say a word. What could I say? There was not one thing I could say to make the pain stop—not one word that would change anything or bring Patsy back. Patsy had said, "God don't give us more than we can bear," but boy, watching Charlie, I wondered, *could* he bear this loss? Seemed like losing Patsy might kill him, too.

I got up off the floor and did what I always do. I got busy. I picked up those beer cans and washed up some dishes—cleaned up things. Got in the kitchen and I finally talked Charlie into eating some real food.

Doolittle arrived after a while and we drove home, both of us quiet the whole way.

Later that night, I sat down at the kitchen table. Doolittle asked if I was all right. I really didn't know for sure. I told him it was like I was just living in a body going through motions. I felt all numb on the inside. Doo, who was always so strong and rarely showed emotion, broke down and started to cry.

"Oh, honey," I said. I wasn't numb then. It warmed me.

Doo held me and said, "I don't know what I would do if I lost you."

I said, "I ain't going anywhere." We held each other for the longest time.

Lonely. That's the word that comes to mind when I think of the weeks after Patsy's death. It was so strange how the sun still rose and set. How our babies still had to get up and go to school and I still had to go on the road and sing. Everyone knew me and Patsy had been good friends, so, from the show promoter to the fans, everybody asked me about her. I didn't really want to talk about it. I wanted a day—one dadgum day—to not feel the ache in my chest from losing my friend. I wanted everything to be like it was before.

Twins in the Family

Patsy had helped me believe that I could have another baby again. So I knew she'd have been over the moon when, in August of 1964, I gave birth to twin girls. Would you believe they were born in the very same hospital in Madison, Tennessee, where I'd met Patsy? It's true! She'd have gotten a kick out of that.

Doo and I laughed, knowing she'd have ribbed him about those twins. She'd have said, "Hell, Mooney, one wasn't enough? You had to go and have two at once?" Or she'd have said, "Mooney Lynn, you better not put those little babies in your rodeo. If I see them on ponies, I will kick your ass!"

I imagined Patsy crying happy tears holding little Patsy, her namesake. I wish we'd gotten to watch those twins grow up together. It would have tickled her how Patsy and Peggy grew up to write songs and sing together. I know Patsy'd have been right there with 'em, cheering 'em on.

We didn't know how we'd do it at first, with six kids at home and two of 'em little babies. I was about at my wits' end when I met a woman named Gloria Land while performing in Arkansas. I loved Gloria right off. She was twenty-eight years old at the time. She was an answer to prayers I didn't even know I was praying. Gloria moved to Nashville to help raise our kids. When Gloria moved in, she became part of the family. I couldn't have done it all without her. I learned you can't do it all by yourself, and that's okay.

Writing My Way Through

When me and Patsy became friends I'd just gotten started in Nashville. We got to spend less than two years together. By the time she died in 1963, I had a manager, a publishing contract, a record deal with Decca, and I was a member of the Grand Ole Opry. My career was taking off. I'd learned a lot in the short time we were together. Most of all, I learned that Patsy believed in me, so I should believe in me, too.

It helped that I had the best producer in the world. Together me and Owen made some great records. After I'd had a couple of hits, some of the best songwriters started pitching me songs. Owen said, "Good lyrics don't always make a hit. It has to be the right song for the singer."

When I finally got to number one it was with a song I wrote called "You Ain't Woman Enough" (1966). Some people say it's a women's lib song. I don't know about that. But I'll tell you how I wrote it. I was playing a show in Missouri someplace. Before the show, my hair in curlers, I was backstage and this young lady came up and she said,

"Are you Loretta?" I said, "Yes." She said she wanted to talk to me. She said, "Look out there—you see that man? That's my husband. And that girl with him, that's his girlfriend." This poor woman had tears in her eyes. I turned to her and I said, "Her? Why, honey, she ain't woman enough to take your man." And that just stuck with me. I went right back and wrote that line down. It was a song for sure. I'd lived it. I knew all about seeing your man and another woman, knowing she thinks she can take him. I know what it's like to feel mad and jealous.

So I wrote that song. It came real natural to me to write it. I played it for Doo first before anybody else. I figured he'd know I was singing mostly about him, and I wondered what he'd say. You know what he said? He said, "That there, honey, that's a hit."

Doo never did get upset about my songs. He was a what-you-see-is-what-you-get kind of person. He never was one to beat around the bush. He didn't take it hard or try and make me not sing the truth. That was a good thing. I reckon my songwriting would have been different if he tried to stop me. It was my life and mine to tell about.

He didn't even get mad when I wrote "Don't Come Home a Drinkin'" (1967). I wrote that with my sister Peggy Sue. I'd lived every word of that song. It made me mad as all get out when Doo came home drunk, lovin' up on me. It came easy to me to write, even though it weren't easy to live. So many women tell me they love that song. They feel the truth in it. Maybe they even get a little backbone when they hear it. It makes me feel strong and good, writing and singing songs like that. It's like helping another girl out, giving her those words to say for herself. That song got banned from some radio stations, but folks loved it. They loved it so much it got to be my next number-one hit.

At first I didn't like it when radio stations wouldn't play my songs they thought were "controversial." To me that was just a four-dollar word for what I'd call honesty. Pretty quick I learned that the fans don't give a shit about "controversy," they just want real. I give 'em real.

Doo's catting around gave me lots of inspiration while I was touring. I wrote "Fist City" (1968) about it. It was my way of saying women should stay away from my man. I sang it with a smile, but you can bet I meant every word. Showing that women could be right mad at each other over a man, well, that was different from what Nashville songwriters imagined women ought to sing. They didn't know what women felt. I did. I liked writing about it, too. Taking nothing and making it into something came easy.

"Your Squaw Is on the Warpath" (1969) was the same way. Some people called it feisty. I just told a story. It came from my heart. From my life. Doo'd been callin' me "squaw" for years whenever I'd get mad at him. 'Course my granddaddy was a full-blooded Cherokee Indian, so I was proud of that. It didn't hurt my feelings. I didn't even know people used that word in a mean way. I was just telling what it feels like to be me. And folks loved it. It was a hit, sure enough.

Girls with Guts

Maybe it helped that I sang with a smile on my face. I smiled singing about how being pregnant with the kids underfoot can be a real pain in the ass. 'Cause what else are you gonna do? Fussin' will only get you so far. "One's on the Way" (1971) was the first single I had that was written by Shel Silverstein, who you might know for his children's books like *Where the Sidewalk Ends* and *The Giving Tree*. He was a real character. He'd follow me around and get to know my voice. Then he'd go out and skulk around and come back with something like "One's on the Way." You'd never of thought Shel Silverstein could make a song that'd be banned. But he was honest in what he wrote. And I liked that.

Controversy didn't slow me down. The CMA voted me Entertainer of the Year in 1972. I was the first woman they ever gave that award. Patsy had predicted I'd earn the Female Vocalist of the Year Award, and that was true. I won that award several times. But being named Entertainer of the Year? That was even better than we could have dreamed up in 1963.

Then in 1973 *Newsweek* did a big story on me. I was the first country star to be on the cover.

I wrote "Rated X" (1974) 'cause it made me so mad when women'd get the short end of the stick when it came to breakups. The men would get off like they were heroes. It was a two-way street, far as I'm concerned. That song got banned, too. See, folks thought "Rated X" was dirty 'cause of the title. But it wasn't. It was the opposite. I was saying a woman ought not to have to feel ashamed just 'cause she had a divorce. Them that have minds "eat up with sin"—it's them that should be ashamed.

If it wasn't for "Rated X," I'd of never met Jack White. But that didn't happen 'til much later.

Shel Silverstein wrote some more songs that I recorded besides "One's on the Way." He was real talented. He had a way of getting in your head. He wrote "Hey Loretta" (1974). I could really sing that one 'cause I was feeling taken for granted. I knew a thing or two about working my fingers to the bone while my man was out catting around. Some people said it was a women's liberation song. I didn't know about that—I just knew how I felt. It was true to me, so I sang it.

"The Pill" (1975)—I didn't ever have the pill. If I had, I wouldn't have had four babies in five years. That song really got people's goat. I don't know why, 'cause when it came out women had had the pill for like twenty years. Preachers was preaching against me. The only difference that made was that it helped sell the record. "The Pill" was banned on a lot of stations. It was still a hit. It was a top-five on country charts and crossed over to pop charts, too.

They said it was shocking for me to sing about birth control. That's a load of bull. I was singing about the freedom that came with being able to be in charge of our bodies. I think it's good to enjoy being a woman with the man I love without worrying! Ain't no shame in that. It didn't hurt my feelings. Kitty Wells was my hero, and her song "It Wasn't God Who Made Honky Tonk Angels" got banned, too. So I was in good company.

Breaking Up with the Wilburn Brothers

Both me and Doo loved the Wilburns like family, but in 1971 we realized our relationship wasn't working anymore. My star was rising just as theirs was falling—fast. The boys were barely holding themselves together. I felt like they were holding me back and holding me down.

As a duo, Teddy and Doyle weren't performing together much anymore—just maybe a few dates a year. Teddy had moved to California. I'd hired a full-time band and Doyle toured with me as my manager. The problem was he drank real hard. He'd drink vodka straight out of the bottle. He drank so much that he had a hard time getting along with himself, much less a bus full of men. It really was sad. Now, I am not bashing Doyle. I'd stayed married to an alcoholic for almost fifty years, but my husband wasn't performing with me and he wasn't in charge of my band and my business. If he had been and acted like that, I'd of broke up with him, too!

The boys did so much for me. They helped me get my career to the next level, for sure. I'd had a single on the charts with "Honky Tonk Girl" before they signed on to manage me, but it was Doyle who called Owen Bradley and talked him into giving me a record contract. It was Teddy who worked with me endlessly on my songs and in the studio. It was the Wilburn Brothers' syndicated TV show that put me in front of thousands of people a week. They were my family and I'd been with them for a whole decade. But it was time to leave, so I jumped. As much as it hurt, I had to. I really believe to this day it was the right thing to do. Doo knew how painful this was, so he called to tell them the news. When he got off the phone, he come back to our bedroom. I cried my eyes out while he held me. It wouldn't be the last time I cried about them boys.

Teddy understood about Doyle's drinking. He knew Doyle was in bad shape. He understood why I'd want to let Doyle go. But as a businessman, he wouldn't let me walk away without a fight. He wanted to control "his" piece of my business. He was angry I was walking away.

A couple weeks later, our attorney called to say the Wil-Helm Agency had filed a lawsuit, suing me for *five million dollars*. I couldn't believe it. I just could not accept that the boys would sue me, and not only sue me, but sue me for five million dollars! Turned out Patsy had it wrong about one thing: I did work for them. All those years ago when we first came to town, Doo and I had signed the contract they gave us, thinking they had my best interests at heart. We were stupid. I'd signed a twenty-five-year contract—what's now referred to as a "lifetime contract." We didn't know any better at the time. I'd have to fight like never before to unravel those bad agreements and to take back control of my own future. God help me.

I remember the day I saw it in the paper. The headline was something like COUNTRY MUSIC SINGER LORETTA LYNN SUED BY WILBURN BROTHERS FOR BREACH OF CONTRACT.

"Oh God, Doo!" I said. "Everybody knows. It's in the papers!" We had a lawyer, but soon we had to get a whole legal team to fight for us. Then we had to hire a PR person just to deal with the press! I stopped answering the phone because people we hardly knew were calling us to ask what was going on. I wasn't gonna talk ugly about the Wilburns. Never.

This was a huge breakthrough. So many artists had been hog-tied by unfair contracts that extend for decades. At the time, it never really crossed my mind that I was a woman fighting a war in a man's world—fighting for my freedom and for my career. I was taking on "the Man." The suits in Nashville figured if I won my freedom, all the artists would want fair deals.

Was it hard? Yes. It was hell. It hurt to be locked in a battle with folks who'd been like family. I was so upset I couldn't eat. I lost so much weight I got down to under a hundred pounds. I had to be hospitalized for nervous breakdowns. At one time I got so depressed I tried to overdose. I am not proud of that. I can't believe I did that. It just goes to show how much I wanted the heartache to be over.

When it came time for the hearing, I had to testify about why I felt I had the right to leave these boys I loved like brothers. I cried, they cried. It was a mess. In the end the judge ruled in my favor. I was released from all agreements other than my publishing. I'd won my freedom. For me it was a huge win, but it came at the price of a good friendship. My friend Doyle continued drinking and died less than six years later.

In spite of this, my career took off like a rocket. In the seventies, I guess I was one of the most famous women in the world. That success didn't stop me from missing Doyle and Teddy, though. I missed them every day. I know they missed me, too. The one good thing is they got to benefit from my success. It was like Patsy said—they'd bet on me and hit the jackpot. Sure-Fire Music earned a lot of money on my catalog. *Coal Miner's Daughter* was certified "gold"—and that was just the first of my records to do that.

Would there be a Loretta Lynn, country music singer, without the Wilburns? I don't know. But I know this: Fighting for my freedom made me the Loretta Lynn I am today. Even though it hurt, I can't regret that. I won't.

I was evolving as an artist and my career was outgrowing what the Wilburn brothers could do for me. Knowing what was right didn't make doing it easier. I had to stand up for myself. Patsy was always tellin' me to do that. Besides, she'd been stuck in a bad deal herself for years before she signed with Decca, and she knew a thing or two about bad contracts. She liked the Wilburns, though. Maybe she'd have said, "You're messing up, Little Gal," but I doubt it. She never let anybody hold her back. More likely she would have said, "You kicked those good ole boys right in the balls!" I can hear her say it in my mind. I just wish I could hear it with my own ears.

If You Want to Keep Your Teeth

It had been years since we lost Patsy, but I still felt protective of her. I wanted to keep her memory alive. It broke my heart that she never got to see how much everyone loved that last album she recorded. She'd put her heart and soul into it, wanting it to be great, and, friends, it was. For a while you couldn't turn on the radio without hearing a Patsy Cline song. I wanted to call her and say, "Patsy! 'Crazy' is number one again this week!" But I couldn't, and that kept rebreaking my heart over and over.

It hurt me when they stopped playin' her records on the radio. I wanted everyone to know about Patsy Cline—who she was and what she meant to country music, as well as to my life and my career. I wanted the world to know about Patsy Cline.

So, of course, I wrote about her in *Coal Miner's Daughter*. That book became a best seller. Everyone in Nashville read it. Heck, just about everyone in America did! Turned out I'd kicked up a big hornets' nest with my Patsy chapter, tellin' about how she helped me with them Cadillac gals. Every last one of them girls denied they'd talked about boycotting me. Guess they just feel guilty. It's okay—it all worked out in the end.

By 1971, I reckon folks thought Patsy had been gone long enough that they could speak ill of the dead. I wasn't putting up with any of that—not then, not now. As I said, when you are my friend and someone talks ugly about you, I will fight for you. By that I mean "Fist City" fight.

It was the night of an awards show and I was with some of the other female singers in a big dressing room we all shared. Some of the younger women started asking me questions about *Coal Miner's Daughter*. One said, "How did you put up with Mooney drinking?" I just told the truth. I said, "I love him." Another said, "Did he really run around on you?" I thought that was rude. Some of their husbands were way worse than Doolittle, so I said, "What's your husband up to?" I was getting hot under the collar, I can tell you. Then they started in on Patsy. At first somebody said, "I loved that song, 'Crazy.'" Then one of them who didn't know Patsy at all said, "She was having an affair with her manager." Then another said, "I heard she'd pick men out of the audience to sleep with after a show." I was trying to ignore the gossip, but then somebody said, "Damn, Loretta, you should have put that in your book!" Friends, I lost it. I was so mad I couldn't even sit still. We were all wearing "falls," which is just a fancy word for wigs and hairpieces that were in style back then. I wanted to rip their falls off and knock the fire out of them! How could they say such mean things about Patsy in front of me?

I got up out of that makeup chair, put both hands on my hips, and said, "You all don't know a damn thing about Patsy Cline or what you're talking about. Y'all just need someone to badmouth. If any one of you dares to open your mouth about Patsy Cline again in this dressing room, I swear I will knock your teeth out. I repeat: *One Word!*" That room went silent. You could've heard a hairpin drop. I sat back down in the chair and finished my hair and makeup. Nobody said a word. Those girls were silent the rest of the time I was there.

I had to smile as I was walking out of that room 'cause I could hear Patsy in my mind saying, "You told 'em, Little Gal!" That night I won ACM Female Vocalist of the Year. Patsy must've smiled when she saw that.

I Remember Patsy

Me and Owen talked for years about how I wanted to sing a medley of Patsy Cline songs in my live shows. Owen liked the idea so much that he hatched a plan. The two of us got together and made a whole album called *I Remember Patsy*. It was like a tribute album, with me singing Patsy's songs. I sang them more country than she would 'cause I could never sing like Patsy, but I sure had a good time with it.

We wanted to do something extra to show her how much we loved her, so we taped ourselves talking about Patsy—both of us just sharing stories, having a good time remembering the friend we loved so much.

One day out at the barn, I went into the vocal booth to sing one of my favorite Patsy Cline songs, "She's Got You" by Hank Cochran. Owen was there at the control board. I'd just started to sing the first few notes when I got chill bumps all up and down my arms. I felt her with me there. It was Patsy.

I said, "Owen, you feel that? Patsy is here with us!"

Owen never much bought into spirits or ghosts or any of that, but he felt it, too. All he said was, "There is *something* in there with you, Loretta, 'cause that is the best you have sang this whole record. Patsy must be happy."

I took a moment and cried. I said out loud in that vocal booth there, "I miss you, Patsy. I miss you so bad." Even Owen got choked up.

We released the album on MCA in 1977. And, sure enough, our recording of "She's Got You" became a number one. I guess Owen was right. Patsy must've liked it.

Coal Miner's Daughter, the Movie

Nobody could tell the story of my life without telling about Patsy. It just wouldn't make sense. So when they started to make *Coal Miner's Daughter* into a movie, I knew she'd be portrayed by somebody in the film. What I didn't know was how it would affect me.

I came on set during filming one day and saw Beverly D'Angelo in costume, ready to play the part of Patsy. For a minute I couldn't breathe. I'd gotten used to seeing Sissy Spacek playing me, but seeing Beverly on that soundstage was different. It hurt me. I felt like it wasn't even a movie anymore—it felt too real. Beverly was so great at playing that part, too great. I wanted to run out of that place as fast as I could. I wanted it to be me and Patsy together on that stage for real—to have that life between us that we didn't get a chance to have. I missed her so damn bad right then, it was unbearable. But then I heard the music. Beverly started singing Patsy Cline's "Crazy." Every actress in *Coal Miner's Daughter* sang their own tracks. I tell you what, Beverly was outstanding. I stood there listening and, all of a sudden, I wasn't upset anymore. I was happy. I felt so proud because I knew that *Coal Miner's Daughter* was going to introduce a whole new generation of fans to Patsy Cline.

And it did! In fact, Bernard Schwartz, our producer, fell so in love with Patsy he went on to make another movie about her life a couple years later, called *Sweet Dreams*. I wasn't crazy over how they portrayed Patsy in that movie, but I was happy that she was getting the notoriety and credit she deserved. I took pride in feeling like I had a part to play in that. I was a little upset when I found out that Bernard was not including a Loretta Lynn character in *Sweet Dreams*, since really the whole idea came from my movie. But in the end, I was kinda happy. The movie *Sweet Dreams* felt so close to *Coal Miner's Daughter*—too close, really, like two hit songs that sound too much alike. Bernard, when asked why he didn't have a Loretta Lynn character in the movie, said he felt like *Coal Miner's Daughter* had covered that already. Maybe it did. The future will tell.

Losing Doo

The time I missed my friend most was when I lost my husband, Doolittle.

We'd been married almost forty-eight years when we moved to Branson, Missouri. It was Doo's idea to move there. It had become a tourist destination—like a Vegas of the Midwest. They had all kinds of music artists and acts there—not just country, either. Moving there meant I could stop traveling and let the fans come to me instead. Settling down sounded great. I thought a move to Branson would be good for us both.

Doo found a theater and a house for us. Then my whole band made the move, as well as my son Ernest Ray, my youngest, Peggy, and my oldest, Betty Sue, and her husband. They all joined us in Branson. The house we bought overlooked the lake. Doo was wild for it. He got a new boat and all kinds of fishing gear. He seemed to have a new lease on life.

But the reality was different than the dream. I had to leave the house early to get to the theater, and then I'd be stuck there until late at night. I hated it. Don't get me wrong—Branson, Missouri, is beautiful. It just wasn't for me. Doo saw I was having a hard time and blamed himself. It wasn't his fault, though.

While I was stuck in the theater all day and half the night, Doolittle was at home drinking. He'd start first thing in the morning and drink himself to sleep at night. Doctors told us Doo had diabetes. That scared me half to death. He had to give himself shots, sometimes twice a day. I begged him to quit drinking, but he couldn't—not even for me.

Doo started getting dizzy. He was tired, too, and had a hard time catching his breath. Finally he saw a doctor and learned he needed a triple bypass right away. We went to Springfield, where they had a really good hospital. Doo was proud but I knew he was scared—mostly scared to leave me. The thought of that terrified me.

Doo made it through the heart surgery fine. I thanked the Lord for that. I got to stay right there with him in the recovery room. Doo and I made plans to leave Branson and never look back. Once he was better we'd make another trip to Alaska. We were talking about that when someone came in to tell us our dear friend Conway Twitty had been brought in and rushed into surgery. I was so shocked and sad. I felt like the wind got knocked right out of me. I got up and promised Doo I'd find out what was going on. I asked around until I finally found Conway's wife, Dee, but Conway'd already been wheeled into surgery. Conway died on the operating table in the same hospital where my Doo was recovering from surgery. It was just too much.

When I told Doo the news, he looked up at the ceiling with those baby-blue eyes and his face turned white. I laid my head in his neck and cried—for Conway and for my husband. After that, Doolittle got worse. We spent a good month in Springfield Hospital before they let us go back to Tennessee. Tennessee was still home. We sold our place in Branson and went home for good.

The doctors were clear: Doo was living on borrowed time. So I stopped touring. I couldn't leave Doo for anything. I made a lot of folks mad at me when I up and quit like that. I'm sorry, but I wasn't wasting one second of my time with Doo.

Diabetes is one of the worst diseases because it destroys your body bit by bit, but it leaves your mind so you know all that is happening to you. That's what happened with Doo. First it took his legs, then his kidneys, then his life. On August 22, 1996, I held him in my arms while he slipped away.

For a while I was completely lost. Even with our kids and grandkids around, nothing could bring me comfort. I was angry and hurt. I left the ranch. I couldn't bear to be in the house we'd shared. I went to a little house we kept in Nashville. I stayed there, thinking it'd be just a few weeks—just to get myself together. I ended up staying for a year.

One day Charlie Dick came to see me. We'd kept Charlie as a friend as long as he lived here on this earth, seeing him every once in a while when we were home from touring. We loved when Charlie visited. Him and Doo would jump back into whatever conversation they'd left off on the last time they had been together. He aggravated the hell out of people with his antics—shoot, sometimes he aggravated the hell out of me—but he'd stuck with me after Patsy passed away and I wasn't giving up on him. He was a good man.

When Charlie came to see me after Doo died, I was really in bad shape. He walked in like I had done at his house when Patsy died. He hollered at the top of his lungs, "Get up, Loretta! I got a record I want you to hear."

I said, "Like hell! Go home, Charlie. I don't want to hear no record."

He said, "Well, I need you to listen to it with me. Just me and you, like old times."

What could I say to that? I slipped into a housecoat and made some coffee. Lord knows when was the last time I actually put on clothes. When I walked into my little living room, Charlie walked over and stuffed a CD into the player. He came back and sat down right beside me on the couch. I started to ask what the devil he was fixing to play, but then I heard Patsy's voice. Patsy was talking.

When I heard her voice, my mouth fell open. I said, "Charlie!"

Charlie said, "Just hush now—let's just listen."

It was a live recording of Patsy's performance at the Cimarron Ballroom in Tulsa, Oklahoma, that MCA was about to release to the public. I remembered how Patsy had gone there just after she was released from the hospital, defying doctor's orders so she could perform for her fans.

We sat there, kind of like I did with Charlie the day we listened to Patsy's new record on that basement floor so many years ago, after she'd passed. Together we listened to Patsy sing her rousing "Come On In" and her sultry "A Poor Man's Roses (Or a Rich Man's Gold)." We heard her talking and bantering with the band and the audience about her recent car wreck. I laughed 'til my belly ached and tears rolled down my face.

You see, Charlie knew what I needed. He'd suffered the same devastating loss of a spouse. He knew I needed my friend Patsy. Now Charlie's passed, too. So many people I've loved are gone. It breaks my heart.

Ghosts

Sometimes my loneliness for Patsy has been so strong it's been like a pain in my chest. I'd give near anything to have her back. But as time has gone by, the ache has subsided some.

As they say, life goes on for the living. God knows I've had a lot to be thankful for. My family gives me more joy than I can say. I've been able to perform for millions of people. I've met presidents and movie stars. I've won lots of awards and sold millions of records. I even had an Oscar-winning movie made of my life.

One of my greatest blessings has been my fans. I love meeting them and hearing their stories of how my songs have touched them. That means the world to me. Not too long after I came out of the fog after Doo died, I went back into the studio and cut *Still Country*. Then I went back on the road. And that saved me from going nuts.

But when life gets really hard, I can lose sight of all those blessings. Like this one time I was playing at a club in Vegas. This was one of many times in my career when I'd been away from home for weeks on end. My health was suffering. I wasn't eating well, and I was feeling tired and wrung out. To be honest, I got to thinking, *I don't have one more performance left in me.* I was feeling really low.

It was time for me to be going out onstage. My knees started shaking like they used to back when I first started out. My band began to play the song I was supposed to walk out to, but the music sounded far away and too loud all at the same time. I was about to turn tail and run when all of a sudden I looked into the audience and there she was. It was Patsy! She was up in the corner there, smiling that half smile of hers, holding a lit cigarette. She nodded at me and I could hear her say, "Go on now, Little Gal. You've got this."

What was I to do? I knew better than to argue with Patsy. I took a deep breath and smiled and walked out. I gave them fans my best performance in a long time. After all these years, Patsy was still looking after me, encouraging me. I'd missed that ole girl.

I reckon I'll see her again, soon enough.

Epilogue

On April 1, 2019, I had my first-ever birthday party. That's right, my first! It mighta been my eighty-seventh birthday, but it was my first party. It was the biggest one you ever saw! It was at the Bridgestone Arena, downtown Nashville, just steps away from the Ryman Auditorium—the start of my life here in Nashville. There was something like seventeen thousand people there. That's some kind of party!

Can you believe I never had a birthday party before? Birthdays and such wasn't a big deal when I was growin' up in Kentucky. Momma'd say, "Hey, Loretta. Today you were born. You're five years old now." When I grew up and moved away, seems like I was always working on my birthday. Lots of times I'd be out on the road, singing. I'd get onstage and say, "Hey, it's my birthday!" 'Course, the crowd would cheer. They loved that I was spending my birthday with them. My fans always was like family to me. I'd go on and keep singing and that was it. Nobody ever made a big deal of it. But that's all right, because we sure made up for it when I turned eighty-seven. I stored up for it my whole life and we blew it out. It took me a week to rest up after that! It was a big shebang.

All kinds of stars sang a bunch of my hit songs. Keith Urban, Kacey Musgraves, Miranda Lambert, Martina McBride, George Strait, Alan Jackson, Margo Price (she sang "One's on the Way" while eight weeks pregnant), my dear friend Tanya Tucker, Darius Rucker, Garth Brooks and Trisha Yearwood, Little Big Town, Lee Ann Womack, and Alison Krauss were just a few of the talented and generous people who came out for me. I could hardly believe it!

Two super girl groups sang that night, too. One was the Pistol Annies and the other was the Highwomen. The Highwomen made their debut that night. The girls in that group are Maren Morris, Brandi Carlile, Amanda Shires, and Natalie Hemby. Any one of them is so talented, but together, friends, that's something. I can't help but think of me and Dolly and Tanya, how we loved each other and loved singing together on *Honky Tonk Angels*.

I had such a good time. What might of made me the proudest was having my family there—grandkids and all. I bet there was over a hundred people just from my family alone. They had seats on the sides of the stage for us. My friend Tim Cobb made sure I had a new outfit and a huge fancy chair to sit in. I wanted to watch the whole show. Most artists came out and sang my songs and did a lot of duets me and Conway sang. My dear Jack White brought out every one of the original players that played on our Grammy-winning *Van Lear Rose* record and sang two songs off it. It was really something.

My good friends Reba McEntire and Dolly Parton sent videos. Dolly was on a movie set and couldn't make it back to Nashville. That meant a lot to me, to have her send that. She knows I love her. She's probably my closest friend in the music business. We've been friends forever. She had a split with Porter Wagoner, back in the day, so she knows the pain of a breakup like mine with the Wilburn brothers. That kind of shared heartache can make you closer. Dolly's really smart and she's kind, too. I never heard her say anything bad about anybody. She never forgot her roots, either. She came from the hills like me. We grew up probably seventy-five miles apart, which is funny. She was probably jerked up by the hair of her head like I was. She tries to give back, too. She's a good person.

At the end of the concert, all the stars and all my family came up and sang "Coal Miner's Daughter" with me. That was real special.

But my favorite moment of the night was probably when Brandi Carlile walked out onstage and sang "She's Got You." Those lyrics hit me like a ton a bricks. "I've got your memory / or has it got me / I really don't know / but I know it won't let me be." Patsy and I both had versions of that song that went to number one—Patsy in the sixties and me in the seventies. Our friend Hank Cochran wrote it for Patsy, and she sang the fire out of it. It was on the last album she recorded. It always got me thinking how true the words were for me. I thought for sure Patsy was there with us when Brandi was singing. I sat there, by the side of the stage, listening to all these amazing singers—so many of them women—holding my grown daughter Patsy's hand, both of us smiling at each other. It was truly full circle for me.

P.S.

Not long ago, my daughter Patsy Russell made me a playlist of my favorite songs on my computer. I really am impressed with how all this new technology has changed how folks listen to music and what they are listening to. I couldn't believe all the songs you could find: From the newest all the way back to the old ones like the Carter Family's "Keep on the Sunny Side." I remember my mommy singing that song to us kids all the time. One of my favorite singers on the playlist is Bob Dylan. His song "Blowin' in the Wind" proves he's one of the greatest songwriters ever. One day I'm gonna record that song.

By now I bet I have close to a thousand songs on my playlist, but at the top is always Patsy Cline, followed by Conway Twitty. These two hold a special place in my heart always.

After readin' this book, if y'all are thinking about listening to some Patsy Cline, and I hope you do, let me tell you the songs I love best. We'll call them my "Patsy Top Ten."

1. "Walkin' After Midnight"
2. "Half As Much As I Love You"
3. "Blue Moon of Kentucky"
4. "Lovesick Blues"
5. "Crazy"
6. "Back in Baby's Arms"
7. "Imagine That"
8. "Fall to Pieces"
9. "She's Got You"
10. "Leavin' on Your Mind"

Now, these are just my top-ten favorites, but, friends, Patsy never sang a bad song—so listen to them all, if you can. I hope reading this book made you feel a little closer to her, kind of like she was your friend, too. When you listen to her music, I hope you feel that same closeness, as if she's singing just for you. The truth is, she was.

Acknowledgments

Thank you to these folks below, who helped me with this book from the beginning:

Special thank you to Ami McConnell—you are such a great writer. You added so much to this book and made it better.

Denise Stevens of Loeb & Loeb—thank you for always thinking of me and looking after me and my business. You helped make this book happen.

Jeff Kleinman and Steve Troha at Folio Literary Management—you boys hung in there with me to the end. Thank you.

David Brokaw, my friend and publicist for over forty years. You have always been there for me. I love you.

And, finally, thank you to Hachette Book Group and the Grand Central Publishing team, who all pitched in to get this book published: our editor, Suzanne O'Neill, and her assistant, Jacqui Young; the publicity team, Jimmy Franco and Alli Rosenthal; marketers Amanda Pritzker,

Andrew Duncan, and Morgan Swift; and production editor Jeff Holt. Thanks to the editor in chief, Karen Kosztolnyik; publisher Ben Sevier; and the CEO of Hachette Book Group, Michael Pietsch.

Loretta Lynn, 2019

Thanks, Mom, for always being my everything. You never fail to let all your children know how much you love us. We've shared so many emotions writing this book—we've laughed, cried, and so deeply missed the ones we lost. Thank you for sharing your friendship with Patsy with me. I am so proud to be her namesake and proud of being a part of this story to share. Deepest thanks to my family: Philip, Kat, Megan, Anthony, Jennafer, Melody, Emmy, David, I love you all more than you know. To my twin, Peggy J. Marchetti, you are my sunshine.

Patsy Lynn Russell, 2019

Index

About the Authors

Loretta Lynn is one of the most storied and celebrated female country artists in the history of country music. Pushing the boundaries at the time, she became a new kind of female country music artist—one that inspires and sets the groundwork for today's biggest names on the music scene.

As millions who read her 1976 autobiography or saw its Oscar-winning 1980 film treatment are aware, Loretta is a coal miner's daughter who was raised in dire poverty in a remote Appalachian hamlet in Kentucky. Living in a mountain cabin with seven brothers and sisters, she was surrounded by music as a child. "I thought everybody sang, because everybody up there in Butcher Holler did," she recalls. "Everybody in my family sang. So I really didn't understand until I left Butcher Holler that there were some people who couldn't. And it was kind of a shock."

She famously married Oliver "Doolittle" Lynn when she was a barely schooled child of fifteen. "Doo" was a twenty-one-year-old war veteran with a reputation as a hell-raiser. By age twenty, Loretta had four children (two more—twins—came along in 1964).

After moving to Nashville in 1960, Loretta, a self-taught guitarist and songwriter, became one of the most distinctive performers in Nashville in the 1960s and 1970s, shaking things up by writing her own songs, many of which tackled boundary-pushing topics drawn from her life experiences as a wife and mother.

Since then, Loretta has recorded multiple gold albums and boasts an impressive sixty-year track record, during which she has sold over forty-five million albums and produced sixteen #1 hit singles and eleven #1 albums. She has received numerous awards and other accolades for her groundbreaking role in country music, including awards from both the Country Music Association and the Academy of Country Music as a duet partner and an individual artist. She is the most awarded female country recording artist and the only female ACM Artist of the Decade (1970s). Loretta continues this celebrated legacy even today, publishing her latest album, *Wouldn't It Be Great*, in 2018.

Patsy Lynn Russell is one of Loretta's daughters, born a year after Patsy Cline's death. She grew up listening to her mother's stories of Patsy Cline. A singer-songwriter and Grammy-nominated music producer in her own right, she has made it her mission to keep her mom's story and legacy alive for future generations of empowered women.